TEXTS THAT TRANSFORM:
Life

Also in this series by the same author:

TEXTS THAT TRANSFORM:
Life

Terry L. Johnson

THE BANNER OF TRUTH TRUST

THE BANNER OF TRUTH TRUST

Head Office
3 Murrayfield Road
Edinburgh, EH12 6EL
UK

North America Sales
610 Alexander Spring Road
Carlisle, PA 17015
USA

banneroftruth.org

First published 2023
© Terry L. Johnson 2023

*

ISBN
Print: 978 1 80040 348 2
Epub: 978 1 80040 349 9

*

Typeset in 11/15 Adobe Garamond Pro
at The Banner of Truth Trust, Edinburgh

Printed in the USA by
Versa Press Inc.,
East Peoria, IL

Contents

Preface

THE following pages lead the reader from text to text that have made a life-changing, life-altering impact on me. I share them in the conviction that 'the word of God is living and active and sharper than any two-edged sword' (Heb. 4:12). The gospel, the gospel itself, is 'the power of God for salvation to everyone who believes' (Rom 1:16). It is the power of regeneration, the power of transformation, the power of change, the power of sanctification, the power of growth, the power of perseverance (John 17:17; Rom. 10:17; 1 Pet. 1:23–2:2). These studies are written in the hope that exposure to these texts will have a similar life-changing impact upon those who read them.

At the heart of this project is a series of sermons preached periodically on Sunday evenings at the Independent Presbyterian Church of Savannah, between July 2016 and January 2022. I am indebted to my two long-suffering secretaries, Mrs Karen Hansill, who served from the beginning of the series until August 2021, painfully transcribing my Bic-pen scribbles into legible and sensible type, and Miss Elise Rustine, who seamlessly moved into Karen's chair, first part-time from January through July of 2021, and then full-time on August 1st, and put the manuscript into final form. May their patience, kindness, and competence be richly rewarded.

Terry L. Johnson
Savannah, Georgia, 2023

Introduction

'LIGHT came in as a flood and all was clear,' said Andrew Carnegie, the great steel industrialist, of his first exposure to evolutionary theory. 'Not only had I got rid of theology and the supernatural, but I found the truth of evolution.' Darwin's 'survival of the fittest' became the driving principle of Carnegie's business practices, as he successfully gobbled up his inferiors and bested his competitors on the way to building the largest steel-producing company in the world.

We tend to underestimate the power of conviction. We elevate feelings to the top of our hierarchy of values. Public radio motivates generous financial support urging 'you'll feel good' for doing so. 'I feel like we should, or shouldn't,' we say, betraying our preference for the emotional over the rational. Yet it is conviction that makes the world go round. The austerity and sacrifice of early Marxists would have been the envy of medieval monks, as they pursued their utopian vision of a workers' paradise. That the Soviet republics and their offshoots became workers' nightmares is beside the point. Conviction drove them to sacrifice worldly comfort and recognition for the sake of their vision of a better world.

Martin Luther (1483–1546) wrestled with the meaning of the phrase 'the righteousness of God' in Romans 1:17 and the meaning of 'the just shall live by faith' in Romans 1:16. One day it came to him.

> Night and day I pondered until I saw the connection between the justice of God and the statement that 'the just shall live by his faith.' Then I grasped that the justice of God is that righteousness by which through grace and sheer mercy God justifies us through faith. Thereupon I felt myself to be reborn and to have gone through open doors into paradise. The whole of Scripture took on a new meaning, and whereas before the 'justice of God' had filled me with hate, now it became to me inexpressibly sweet in greater love. This passage of Paul became a gate to heaven…'[1]

Luther's life was transformed and his world upended by the power of this insight, as he posted his Ninety-five Theses and launched the Protestant Reformation.

Conviction

The Holy Spirit has used a number of key verses to transform my outlook and alter the course of my life. Time and again this has proven to be the case for me. The gospel is the power of God (Rom. 1:16). Scriptural truth has at times erupted into my consciousness like a volcano, at other times

---

[1] Roland H. Bainton, *Here I Stand: A Life of Martin Luther* (New York: Penguin Group, 1995), 36.

slowly melted away my misconceptions and objections like butter on a warm skillet. New convictions came to replace the old, sometimes like a flood, sometimes like the dripping of a faucet. Jesus Christ has changed my life in stages, by his Spirit working through his word. Mine has been a text-driven life. My personal experience of conviction-wrought change has given shape to everything I have gone on to do in ministry: from *lectio continua* (verse by verse) preaching to doctrinally-driven Inquirers' classes to catechizing our children. I have aimed at conviction in others. I have sought, as did the apostle Paul before me, to *persuade*, persuade by reasoning and explaining from the Scriptures (Acts 17:2-4; 18:4; 19:9).

1

One Way

JOHN 14:6

Jesus said to him, 'I am the way, and the truth, and the life. No one comes to the Father except through me.'

I WAS reared in a solidly Christian home. My two older sisters (Gail and Peggy) and I were in Sunday School and church every Sunday. The services we attended throughout our childhood and youth were evangelistic. We heard the gospel preached every Sunday morning and every Sunday night. I am grateful for this heritage and the impact it made on me from the beginning of my life.

In particular, John 3:16 made an early impact, setting the stage, as it were, for John 14:6. This was the first verse that I memorized (as was the case for church-going children of my generation, in the Authorised or King James Version of course): 'For God so loved the world, that he gave his only begotten Son, that whosoever believeth in him should not perish, but have everlasting life.'

'Here is gospel indeed,' says Matthew Henry (1662–1714), 'the best that ever came from heaven to earth.'[1] I cannot remember a time when I did not believe John 3:16. It presents the whole gospel. God loved the world. God gave his only Son, Jesus, to die for our sins. Those who believe are saved. They are given eternal, or 'everlasting life.' Those who don't believe 'perish.' Humanity is a perishing condition. We need rescue. We need a deliverer. We need a saviour. Jesus is that God-given Saviour. Belief is 'the great gospel duty,' says Henry.[2] I never doubted that John 3:16 was true. Later came exposure to John 14:6. Jesus responds to a perplexed Phillip, 'I am the way, and the truth, and the life. No one comes to the Father except through me.'

Moral and religious relativism was all the rage in the revolutionary 1960s. What is right is right for you, we are assured. What is true is true for you. There are many paths leading to the same mountaintop, etc. Then came the Jesus Movement and its slogan was: 'one way!' Complete with upraised index finger. Christian bumper stickers proliferated in those days, leading to the not-uncommon sight of drivers on the Southern California freeways signalling 'one way' to each other while rushing to work at 65 mph in bumper to bumper traffic.[3]

---

[1] Matthew Henry, *An Exposition of the Old and New Testaments* (1708–10, various editions), on John 3:16.

[2] *Ibid.*

[3] See Larry Eskridge, *God's Forever Family* (New York: Oxford University Press, 2013), for an excellent survey of the movement.

I became convinced at an early age that Jesus is the only way of salvation. I don't remember ever not believing that there is 'salvation in no one else' (Acts 4:12). An early sermon on hell proved particularly motivational. Heaven and hell, life and death, eternity and time, light and darkness, truth and error were all absolute categories for me at a very early age. For these formative convictions, I am eternally grateful to my family and churches I attended in my childhood and youth.

At the age of fourteen I stood in the bathroom brushing my teeth when I silently, internally shouted, 'Okay, I surrender.' I had resisted yielding to the will of God up to that point, fearing he'd send me to the proverbial grass hut amongst stone-age tribes. At that strange moment, toothbrush in mouth, looking into the mirror, I caved. Two weeks later I was baptized. John 14:6 played a crucial role in solidifying my convictions. Three nouns and three definite articles. It's hard to escape the implications. It's hard to relativize the emphatic. I am *the* way, not *a* way but the one and only way, *the* truth, not *a* truth, but the singular truth, and *the* light, the one and only light. 'Great things Christ here saith of himself,' says Henry.[4] Indeed he has. Jesus is gracious to the thickheaded and hardhearted by adding to his positive affirmation an emphatic negative restatement: 'No one comes to the Father but by me.' No one. No other path. No other saviour. Only *by me*.

[4] Henry, *Exposition*, on John 14:6.

What these childhood convictions and youthful commitments meant in practice was that I was always, it seems, conscious that others need Christ and salvation. I carried a burden for the lost.

Whether or not I was kind or mean, truthful or deceiving, loving or hateful, bold or timid might make the difference for some lost soul. Convictions from John 3:16 and 14:6 led inevitably to mission.

Witness

I recall having one of my boyhood friends spend the night. We turned out the lights. I felt convicted that I needed to ask him if he believed. I paused. Finally I got up the nerve. 'Do you believe in Jesus?' I asked. A long silence followed. Finally, out of the darkness a weak voice said, 'Yes.' That was the end of it. I had no idea of what to say next. Yet I was concerned about his soul and I had to ask.

I was the ringleader in my youth group, asking, begging, pleading with my circle of friends to get involved. Most of them did. I used to badger our youth director to teach a lesson. (He had a bad habit of telling jokes the whole Sunday School hour.) Why? Two reasons. I was concerned for the salvation of my friends. Why? John 3:16. Apart from Jesus they were perishing. Eternal life was there for the asking. Why the concern? John 14:6. I believed in heaven and hell. I believed that Jesus was the only way. I wanted my friends to be saved. I didn't want them to spend eternity in hell. Conviction gave rise to a personal sense of responsibility.

I was privileged to know the truth. The privilege carried a responsibility to tell others. I could not be silent. It would be irresponsible. Mine were not the highest motivations, yet they were valid motivations: concern for lost souls, and my responsibilities for them.

Motivation

Biblical, theological convictions are critical in motivating believers. Faith alone, in Jesus alone, saves. At times even unbelievers seem to understand the connection between conviction and outreach. Some time ago, an article in *The Atlantic* cited Michael, a Dartmouth student and atheist, who said, 'I really can't consider a Christian a good, moral person if he isn't trying to convert me.' Similarly, Penn Jillette, the atheist illusionist and comedian, said,

> I don't respect people who don't proselytize. I don't respect that at all. If you believe that there's a heaven and hell and people could be going to hell or not getting eternal life or whatever, and you think that it's not really worth telling them this because it would make it socially awkward … How much do you have to hate somebody to believe that everlasting life is possible and not tell them that?

Michael's words are worth pondering: 'Christianity is something that if you really believed it, it would change your life and you would want to change [the lives] of others. I haven't seen too much of that.'[5]

[5] Larry Alex Taunton, 'Listening to Young Atheists: Lessons for a Stronger Christianity,' *The Atlantic*, June 5, 2013.

Don't underestimate the role of convictions in changing lives. Becoming convinced that the gospel is true is a vital step in motivating Christian ministry: outreach, witness, evangelism, church-planting, and world missions. Why do we expend so much energy, time and treasure in these endeavours? Because we are convinced that Jesus Christ is *the* way, *the* truth, and *the* life, and that we can only come to the Father through him. Let this truth sink into our souls and we will find it affecting every aspect of our lives, 'taking every thought captive,' as the apostle Paul might say, that sinners might be saved (2 Cor. 10:5).

2

Justifying the Ungodly

ROMANS 4:1-5

And to the one who does not work but believes in him who justifies the ungodly, his faith is counted as righteousness.

THE Baptist church of my youth used the revival meeting format for its morning worship service. The service begins with the first and last stanzas of favourite gospel songs led by a gregarious 'song leader' (these were pre-'worship leader' days). Offering—Special Music—Sermon—Altar Call— Multiple verses of 'Just as I Am.' The deacons would then go out and have a smoke.

I heard the gospel call to repentance and faith in Christ on *every single Sunday*. Never, not once, not for a moment did I ever believe that one could be saved except through faith in Jesus, apart from any works. That was clear. Good works could never get a person into heaven.

Yet, as a teenager I became highly uncomfortable with

what I later heard called 'easy-believism.' Scores of people in our ecclesiastical circle had walked the aisle, prayed the 'sinner's prayer,' were born again and saved, and yet never showed the least sign of authentic Christianity. They were immoral. They had foul mouths. They were drunks. They were mean. They were proud. Yet they had assurance. Oh yes. They knew they were saved. I may have been a mushy-headed teenager, but I knew something was wrong with *that*. The real gospel changes people. Too many people weren't changed.

I grew rapidly in my faith during my sophomore and ensuing years of college. As I matured, I became even more troubled by the 'cheap-grace' evangelicalism seen everywhere in Southern California. I had bumped into James and 'faith without works is dead,' heightening my confusion (James 2:26). However, I continued to devour my Bible. One day I came to this verse: 'But to the one who does not work, but believes in him who justifies the ungodly, his faith is credited as righteousness' (Rom. 4:5, NASB). Here was the confirmation of my childhood evangelical faith. The apostle's subject is Abraham's salvation as an illustration of the salvation of which he had been writing in the immediately preceding paragraph: justification by grace alone through faith in Christ alone, faith in his atoning, propitiating sacrifice apart from works of the law (Rom. 3:24-28). He now writes, 'For if Abraham was justified by works, he has something to boast about, but not before God' (Rom. 4:2).

Notice the connection between boasting and works. If my religious works and moral behaviour earn salvation, I might boast of my accomplishments. 'Look at how moral I am, how religious, how devout.' Surely, one might think, if anyone is to get into heaven, I will. Not so with Abraham, and not so 'before God.' Rather than salvation through works about which Abraham might boast, he was justified by faith. 'For what does the Scripture say? "Abraham believed God, and it was counted to him as righteousness"' (Rom. 4:3).

The apostle's citations from Genesis 15:6 are a clear Old Testament statement of salvation by faith. Abraham was instructed to look at the stars of heaven and promised 'so shall your descendants be' (Gen. 15:5, NASB). Abraham's response: 'He believed the Lord and he counted it to him as righteousness' (Gen. 15:5, 6). Right then and there, before he could do any good works, God counted him as righteous on the basis of faith alone. Then Paul contrasts the principle of works and its necessary wages (earnings, merits) with faith and its gift. 'Now to the one who works, his wages are not counted as a gift but as his due' (Rom. 4:4).

When I carried furniture up and down steps, in and out of houses, all day long during my college summers, my paycheck was not a gift from the owner of the moving van and storage company. My 'wages' were not 'counted as a gift, but as (my) dues!' He owed me that check. This is exactly what salvation is *not*.

Finally, the apostle clinches his argument: 'And to the one who does not work but believes in him who justifies the ungodly, his faith is counted as righteousness' (Rom. 4:5). Could the graciousness of the gospel possibly be stated more clearly?

'Does not work'

What is necessary for salvation? The apostle has already concluded that 'every mouth' is 'closed' to all self-justifying claims or excuses. All of us, whether Jews who have the law or Gentiles who don't, are 'accountable' and condemned. The law condemns the 'whole world' (Rom. 3:19, NASB, summarizing Rom. 1:18–3:18). 'All have sinned and fall short of the glory of God' (Rom. 3:23). How do we escape? 'The one who *does not work.*' Works are not only *not required*, they are *excluded.* Works are given no consideration, no place, no credit in relation to justification/salvation. One must 'not work,' that is, one must not attribute any meritorious value to good deeds whatsoever. Salvation is '*not a result of works*' (Eph. 2:9; 2 Tim. 1:9). When our Saviour appeared, says the apostle again, 'he saved us, *not because of works* done by us in righteousness, but according to his own mercy' (Titus 3:4, 5). Once more: 'A person is *not justified by the works of the law* … because by works of the law no one will be justified' (Gal. 2:16).

If it were the case that we are saved by the works of the law, by good moral and religious habits, then 'grace would no longer be grace' (Rom. 11:6). Grace would be replaced by justice and merit if salvation were by works and law. The whole gospel would be lost in the process, which is why the apostle Paul calls any compromising of the grace-faith principle 'a different gospel' which is not really another, but a 'contrary' gospel, and pronounces curses upon it (Gal. 1:6-9). Then we would get only what we earned and merited, and no more. Given that we could never sufficiently earn or merit anything from God, we would be hopelessly lost, which is exactly what the Bible teaches we are apart from Christ (Eph. 2:12). 'A man gets to heaven by works?' the great evangelist George Whitefield (1714–70) once asked. 'I should as soon think of climbing to the moon on a rope of sand.'

'Believes in him'

What is necessary for salvation? One need only 'believe.' 'What must I do to be saved?' 'Believe on the Lord Jesus, and you will be saved' (Acts 16:30). One must only have 'faith' in Jesus Christ, his cross, his atonement, his victorious resurrection, and one is saved. The texts cited above concur. 'By grace you have been saved through *faith*' (Eph. 2:8). A person is justified 'through *faith* in Jesus Christ, so also we have believed in Christ Jesus in order to be justified by *faith* in Christ' (Gal. 2:16). We have not 'a righteousness of (our) own that comes through the law, but that which comes through *faith* in Christ, the righteousness from God that depends on *faith*' (Phil. 3:9). Back to the book of Romans: 'For we hold that one is justified by faith apart from works of the law' (3:28).

How do I receive the benefit of Jesus' life, death, and resurrection? I need only open the empty hands of faith and receive it as a gift. Salvation 'is the *gift* of God' (Eph. 2:8, 9). 'The free *gift* of God is eternal life through Christ Jesus our Lord' (Rom. 6:23). This leads to our next point.

'Who justifies the ungodly'

The gospel message gets better. One's faith is in the God who 'justifies the ungodly.' 'Justifies' is the language of the courtroom. To be justified is to be considered 'not guilty,' even innocent in God's court. The Judge's verdict is that we are righteous. Who is justified? The *ungodly*, while still ungodly. They don't first clean up their act, or straighten up their lives, or turn over a new leaf. They merely look to Christ and his cross. Though they are still 'ungodly,' they are 'reckoned' or 'counted' as 'righteous.' They're not righteous. Yet they, the ungodly, though still ungodly, are considered righteous in Christ. The righteousness of Christ is imputed or credited to them. We receive what Luther called 'an alien righteousness' (*justitia aliena*), a righteousness foreign to us and outside of us.[1] We are rendered, said Luther again, *simul jus et precator*, at once just (by God's verdict) and sinner (by

---

[1] Martin Luther, 'Two Kinds of Righteousness,' in T. F. Lull, (ed.), *Martin Luther's Theological Writings* (Minneapolis: Fortress Press, 1989), 157.

nature and practice).[2] The gospel reveals not a righteousness that we achieve through moral and religious deeds, but a righteousness 'of God,' meaning 'from God,' received as a gift (Rom. 1:16, 17). It is a 'righteousness of God through faith in Jesus Christ for all who believe' (Rom. 3:22). In Christ we have a righteousness that is not our own, 'that comes from the law, but that which comes through faith in Christ, the righteousness *from* God that depends on faith' (Phil. 3:9, 10).

'Counted as righteousness'

'Counted' or 'reckoned' is an accounting term. The faith of the ungodly is counted or considered as righteousness. There are two sides to justification. There is both the negative and the positive. Debts are removed and assets are deposited. Christ bears our sin, eliminating our debt of sin, taking our spiritual bank account back to zero. Yet it doesn't remain at zero. We are credited with a vast, even infinite sum of righteousness, Christ's own righteousness. Guilt is removed by the cross, and an infinite treasure of righteousness is credited. Jesus 'fulfilled all righteousness' (Matt. 3:15). The righteousness of his perfectly righteous life is credited to

---

[2] 'A Christian man is both righteous and a sinner, holy and profane, an enemy of God and yet a child of God' (227), 'counted righteous, though sins notwithstanding do remain in us, and that great sins … a Christian is righteous and beloved of God, and yet notwithstanding he is a sinner' (Martin Luther, *Commentary on St Paul's Epistle to the Galatians* [1575; repr. New York: Robert Carter, 1844], 229).

us, even as 'He made him who knew no sin to be sin,' that is, to bear the guilt of our sin, 'that we might be the righteousness of God in him' (2 Cor 5:21, NASB).

Back at college I read Romans 4:5 to a confused sorority girl at a social event, pausing on each word: *who does not work but believes*, my voice rising with enthusiasm. It's wonderful, isn't it?! Salvation is free. It is a gift. It is all of grace. It is all of Christ. We may well understand why Luther would refer to this arrangement as a 'wonderful exchange.'[3]

The *sola fide* part of my unrest was nailed down, closed, shut, never to be reopened. I wasn't entirely sure of what to do with works considered positively. Jesus says others are to see our 'good works' and 'glorify (our) Father in heaven' (Matt. 5:16, NASB). We are to be 'zealous for good works,' says the apostle (Titus 2:14). Concern about works will have to await another study. Yet, a critical hurdle in understanding had been cleared and the graciousness of the gospel was unshakably grasped, with floods of accompanying gratitude and relief, not to mention motivation to spread the good news around.

---

[3] Cited in J. I. Packer, *Collected Shorter Writings of J. I. Packer: Honouring the People of God*, vols 1-4 (Carlisle, Cumbria, UK: Paternoster Press, 1999), 4:225; cited from Luther, *Commentary on the Psalms*, *Luther's Works*, V:608.

3

The Romans Road

ROMANS 10:1-13

*For the wages of sin is death, but the free gift of God is
eternal life in Christ Jesus our Lord* (Rom. 6:23).

IT has long been recognized that the apostle Paul's Epistle
to the Romans is the most systematic presentation of the
gospel found in the Bible. Following his introduction (1:1-
17), the apostle takes up his subject logically from the human
problem: the universality of sin (1:18–3:20); to the solution:
Christ, the cross, and justification by faith (3:21–5:21). From
there he deals with new life in union with Christ (ch. 6);
the continuing struggle with the remnants of sin (ch. 7);
the indwelling Spirit of adoption (ch. 8); election (ch. 9–11),
and practical aspects of the Christian life (ch. 12–16).

This systematic presentation of Christ and his work
lends itself to easy adaptation. Those looking for a logi-
cal, biblical, convenient tool for sharing the core of the
gospel with unbelievers need look no further. Hence some

unnamed person devised 'The Romans Road,' a series of 4–6 key verses (depending on if one were utilizing the extended or contracted version). The Romans Road was important to me in my mid to late teens, as it helped me both with personal assurance and with witness to others. Should we not be ambassadors of Christ, representing him to the world, telling others of salvation through his cross (2 Cor. 5:20)? Exposure to the Romans Road may help us to be more effective as Christian witnesses.

The problem

> *For all have sinned and fall short of the glory of God* (Rom. 3:23).

What is the human condition?

'All have sinned,' says the apostle. Sin is universal. No one is free from its stain. No one is free from its corruption. All have sinned, that is, have violated God's laws (1 John 3:4).[1] 'All … fall short of the glory of God.' Sin is both inherited and personal. We are guilty in Adam, as his guilty status is passed down to his descendants. 'One trespass led to condemnation for all men' (Rom. 5:18). Also passed down was Adam's corrupt nature: 'By the one man's disobedience the many were made sinners' (Rom. 5:19). 'Original sin' consists in both original guilt and original corruption. We are born under both the penalty and power of sin, and

---

[1] 'Sin is any want of conformity unto, or transgression of, the law of God' (*Shorter Catechism*, Q. 14). 'Sin is lawlessness' (1 John 3:4).

consequently we are both hopelessly and helplessly lost (biblical words: Eph. 2:12; Rom. 5:6). We are 'dead in our trespasses and sins' (Eph. 2:1).

All that is wrong in the world may be traced to this source. All the hate, all the crime, all the oppression, all the neglect of the needy, all the violence, all the conflict, all the war are a direct result of humanity's guilt and corruption. My personal evils, my anger, my hatred, my pride, my covetousness, my extraordinary selfishness and self-centredness are all a direct result of humanity's fall. More or less this is what was explained to me in my childhood and youth. 'Jesus saves' was an empty phrase without this preliminary explanation of the context of his death. Well-meaning Christians who wrote these words on a college library desktop at the University of Southern California provoked two responses: first, 'Jesus wouldn't write on desktops,' and second, 'Moses invests.' 'Jesus saves,' but from what? 'Jesus is the answer,' but what is the question? Why did he die? Romans 3:23 provides the first step in our answer: 'All have sinned.'

The consequence

> The wages of sin is death (Rom. 6:23).

Our inherited guilt plus the accumulated guilt of our own 'actual transgressions' (in the language of the *Westminster Confession of Faith*) means death. This was the warning to our first parents in the garden: 'The day that you eat of it you will die' (Gen. 2:17). So they did. They ate and died, immediately spiritually, then later physically. Death entered the world through sin and 'death spread to all men' (Rom. 5:13). Death and all the lesser deaths of sickness, injuries, disabilities, suffering, and sorrow are all the consequence of the sin and guilt from which we cannot rescue ourselves. Physical death awaits us, and beyond it, eternal death in hell, 'where the worm does not die and the fire is not quenched' (Mark 9:48). This is what I needed to know. I needed to know my problem and the consequence. I needed a correct diagnosis. I needed to know where I stood with God. I needed to know of the disapproval of a holy God, of his wrath against sin, of the judgment to come, and my certain everlasting doom.

The remedy

> *God shows his love for us in that while we were still sinners, Christ died for us* (Rom. 5:8).
>
> *The free gift of God is eternal life in Christ Jesus our Lord* (Rom. 6:23).

God is love (1 John 4:8). God demonstrated that he is love by sending his blessed and eternal Son to die 'for us,' that is, as our substitute in our place, in our stead, on our behalf, dying our death, paying our debt (Rom. 5:8). His was a blood sacrifice, a substitutionary atonement, a propitiatory sacrifice, one which satisfied the requirements of divine justice and so put away divine wrath (Rom. 3:25; 1 John 2:2). He is 'the lamb of God,' the sacrificial lamb, the

Passover lamb 'who takes away the sin of the world' (John 1:29). He gave his life as a 'ransom' for us (Mark 10:45). His death achieves 'redemption,' the price paid to liberate slaves from bondage (Rom. 3:24; 1 Cor. 1:30; Eph. 1:7; Col. 1:4; Heb. 9:15). His death was final and complete, 'one sacrifice for sins for all time' (Heb. 10:12, NASB; cf. Heb. 7:27). Or, as Jesus affirmed the finality and sufficiency of his sacrifice with eloquent simplicity, 'It is finished' (John 19:30).

Where was I to look for salvation? Was I to trust in the universal benevolence of God, as were so many of my contemporaries? ('It is his job to forgive,' they said. 'A loving God would never condemn us to hell,' they were sure.) Was I to look to my own virtues, or good conduct ('I'm a good person'), or religious practices ('I never miss church' or the more recent version, 'I'm a spiritual person')? The emphatic answer of the faithful travellers of the Romans Road was to look only to Christ and his cross. Trust in no one (not even yourself) and nothing but Christ and his once-for-all sacrifice for sin.

Response

> *If you confess with your mouth that Jesus is Lord and believe in your heart that God raised him from the dead, you will be saved. For with the heart one believes and is justified, and with the mouth one confesses and is saved* (Rom. 10:9, 10).

If Jesus by his death 'paid it all,' as we sing in the old gospel song, how do I receive the benefit of his death? What

Jesus did on the cross took place long ago and far away. How do his accomplishments span all that space and time to arrive in the present where I can benefit from them? The answer is, through the gospel message received by faith. When we 'believe in our hearts,' this is our private conviction that 'God raised Jesus from the dead'; and 'confess with our mouths,' this is our public declaration of belief that 'Jesus is Lord'; then 'we will be saved.' What hoops must I jump through? What good works must I perform? None whatever. If one believes from the heart, one is 'justified.' The judicial verdict of condemnation is reversed. A new verdict is declared whereby guilt is removed and righteousness is credited, or 'imputed,' as the theologians would say. Because 'Jesus paid it all,' we contribute nothing but empty, believing hands to receive God's 'free gift' of 'eternal life' (Rom. 6:23).

What about our good works? What about our careful obedience? What about our love for others, our religious devotion? They contribute not 'one single straw,' as John Calvin (1509–64) said.[2] Listen again to the apostle:

> *For by grace you have been saved through faith. And this is not your own doing; it is the gift of God, not a result of works, so that no one may boast* (Eph. 2:8, 9).

Salvation is by 'grace,' not merit; 'faith,' not works; a 'gift of God,' not earned. Because it is a gift and not an

---

[2] John C. Olin (ed.), *A Reformation Debate: John Calvin and Jacopo Sadoleto* (Grand Rapids: Baker Book House, 1966, 1976), 67.

accomplishment for which one can take credit, it excludes boasting (see 1 Cor. 1:29-31; Rom. 4:2-5). Christ is the Saviour only for those who are not seeking to save themselves (Gal. 1:6-9; 5:2-4). I needed to hear this as a young person with tendencies toward self-righteousness and pride. We all need to hear this. I am glad that the Romans Road makes clear to all the graciousness of salvation. Wherever I may lie on the sin spectrum from degraded sinner, in bondage to the darkest, the most corrupt and perverted of sins, or self-righteous, moral, proud pharisaic sinner, salvation is for me a free gift of Christ. This is the gospel's good news.

Continuing story

> How are they to hear without someone preaching? And how are they to preach unless they are sent? As it is written, 'How beautiful are the feet of those who preach the good news!' So faith comes from hearing, and hearing through the word of Christ (Rom. 10:14, 15, 17).

What do I do now that I am a Christian? How do I go on in the Christian life? The above verses are about the church. Preachers don't commission and send themselves. The apostle doesn't say, 'How are they to preach unless they go?' The church is the sending agency by which preachers 'are sent.' It is under its ministry that the word is heard and faith is engendered and confession made. If one is to grow as a Christian, to mature into spiritual adulthood, one must unite with a faithful church and sit under the ministry of the word. Some of us will be among those called to go, and will be sent to exercise this ministry. Others of us will participate in their going by membership in the church by which they are sent. Jesus prayed that we would be sanctified by the truth. What truth? 'Thy word is truth' (John 17:17, KJV).

This too, I needed to hear. We will have much more to say about the church later. For now, let me point out that as a college student, I was surrounded by believers who had minimized the role of the church to the point of total irrelevancy. Yet Jesus said, 'I will build my church' (Matt. 16:18). It is the only entity on earth that he promises to build. The church that he builds is an institution, as is clear from Matthew 18:15ff. 'Tell it to the church.' A church is an entity to which problems can be told and whose voice can be heard. It is an entity with a form of government, a system of discipline, standards of belief and conduct, with officers, and with a mission or purpose. It is not an *ad hoc*, informal, casual, self-selecting group of believers who decide to gather in a coffee shop when convenient. The church is a covenantal community where promises are made and where we are responsible for each other, accountable to each other, and will be there for each other. This is the environment that God has designed and in which we are to thrive until God takes us home.

Have you walked the Romans Road?

Has your self-awareness travelled from the problem (*sin*) to the salvation (*Christ*) to the response (*faith*) to the church (*public profession of Christ and participation in its life and ministry*)?

Those of us who have walked this road, are we ready to lead others down it, from verse to verse to Christ and his church?

Are we ready and willing at least, to say with Philip, 'Come and see' (John 1:46), come to my church where you will hear the way of salvation in Jesus the Messiah, and begin to contribute with us in his great mission?

4

The Great Invitation

MATTHEW 11:28-30

Come to me, all who labour and are heavy laden, and I will give you rest. Take my yoke upon you, and learn from me, for I am gentle and lowly in heart, and you will find rest for your souls. For my yoke is easy, and my burden is light.

'OF course nothing can compete with the 9th,' I wrote to a friend, closing an email exchange about great music. Immediately he shot back, 'Which 9th?' I was incredulous. 'Beethoven's,' I answered. 'Is there any other?' 'Mahler's 9th Symphony,' he immediately answered. Mahler? Gustav Mahler? Sorry … I don't get it. Yet he does. He loves Mahler.

Why is it that some music resonates with one person and not with another? Why does a given speech motivate one person and leave another untouched? Why does one artist's work inspire while others remain unmoved? My father brought home 78rpm album sets of Beethoven's nine symphonies when I was in junior high school. I immediately loved, loved passionately the Great One's 5th Symphony, the 2nd movement of the 7th Symphony, and the 2nd and 4th movements of the 9th Symphony. The passion and power of Beethoven's music deeply moved my young soul.

Let me clarify lest you be misled. I wasn't a complete dork. I also loved the Beatles and the Beach Boys, Boston and the Bee Gees (I had a decided preference for the 'Bs'), Simon and Garfunkel, Cosby, Stills, Nash, and Young, Chicago, the Carpenters (I earned some scorn from the boys on that one), Elton John, and lots of other late 60s to mid-80s popular music. Still, Beethoven was in a class of his own, followed closely by Bach (yet another 'B').

The same curious phenomena of what resonates seems to occur in believing circles regarding the impact of a given sermon, passage, or verse. I recall an elderly man in the hospital passionately reciting Psalm 84:10 (KJV):

> *For a day in thy courts is better than a thousand. I had rather be a doorkeeper in the house of my God, than to dwell in the tents of wickedness.*

Another memorable moment came when one of our deacons at the Tuesday morning prayer meeting led out with great earnestness, 'O LORD, our Lord, how excellent is your name in all the earth' (Psa. 8:1). Clearly he had been touched by that verse. In the spiritual realm we may attribute this difference not to mere aesthetics, but to the work of the

Holy Spirit. Jesus' 'Great Invitation' was such a verse for me. It resonates. It inspires. It moves me. It opens a window into the heart of Christ in a way that little else does. Nowhere 'is the veil so fully lifted from the Redeemer's soul, and his inmost thoughts and deepest emotions more affectionately described, than here,' says the nineteenth-century Scot, David Brown (1803–97).[1]

Come unto me

The sheer openness of his invitation stirs my soul. 'Come unto me,' he urges one and all (KJV). None are excluded. He doesn't qualify who may come. He doesn't disqualify who may not. 'Come unto me all,' he says, without discrimination. The rich and poor, the religious and irreligious, the moral and immoral, are all extended this most gracious of invitations. He doesn't ask for promises. He doesn't require that we get our life together. He doesn't demand that we clean up our act. He simply says, 'Come.' This is biblical religion. This is the gospel. This is the God of the Bible. 'Come,' he says.

The Spirit and the Bride say, 'Come.' And let the one who hears say, 'Come.' And let the one who is thirsty come; let the one who desires take the water of life without price (Rev. 22:17; cf. Isa. 55:1, 2).

---

[1] David Brown, *The Four Gospels: A Commentary, Critical, Experimental, and Practical*, Geneva Series of Commentaries (repr.; Edinburgh: Banner of Truth Trust, 1998), 68.

'*Whosoever*' (KJV), or '*Everyone* who calls on the name of the Lord will be saved' (Rom. 10:13). 'Come unto me *all*' expresses what the theologians have called 'the universal offer of the gospel.' The most degraded of sinners, his life in ruins from a lifetime of evil, the most self-righteous of hypocrites and everyone in between these two, are urged by Jesus to come to him.

Weary and heavy-laden

While Jesus does not demand conditions to meet, he does describe motives to come. We are to come because we are conscious of labouring under a heavy burden, or being 'weary and heavy-laden' with sin (NASB; KJV). He speaks not of physical weariness *per se*, though that may be a consequence of the pursuit of illicit honours, pleasures, and things. Rather what primarily is intended is weariness of soul, the opposite of rest for the soul (verse 29). He welcomes those who are burdened by sin, 'both the guilt and power of it,' says Matthew Henry.[2] Sin weighs us down. 'The way of transgressors is hard,' the Proverbs warn us (13:15, KJV). David describes the impact of sin when indulged in the 32nd Psalm:

> For when I kept silent, my bones wasted away through my groaning all day long. For day and night your hand was heavy upon me; my strength was dried up as by the heat of summer (Psa. 32:3, 4).

[2] Henry, *Exposition*, on Matthew 11:28.

Guilt brings the heavy hand of God down upon the soul. Bones waste away. Guilt eats away at the conscience. Guilt absorbs our strength, sucking the life out of us. A life of sin, of trying and failing to do what is right, as well as a life of defiant rebellion against God's authority, brings weariness and weight upon one's existence. 'The wicked,' says Isaiah, 'are like the tossing sea; for it cannot be quiet, and its waters toss up mire and dirt.' There is a restlessness among the unbelieving. Their souls are ever churning, perpetually unsettled. Sin stirs up anxiety. Sin stirs up fear. Sin stirs up envy and jealousy. Sin stirs up hate. Sin stirs up restlessness and discontent. It wearies and burdens the soul. It exhausts the soul in its pursuit of ever-evasive happiness, fulfilment and satisfaction. 'There is no peace for the wicked' (Isa. 57:20, 21). How does Jesus regard all such? He is tender-hearted and merciful. He says, 'Come.' He's not repulsed by a soul soiled by sin. He is not threatening the soul sold out to sin's pleasures. He is not scary. He is not intimidating. He is welcoming. He is eager to help, ready to serve, eager to save.

I will give you rest

What can Jesus do for the weary and heavy-laden? We see that he is willing to rescue us. However, is he able? Indeed. He can provide rest for our souls. For all souls. For every soul. It is a remarkable claim. 'I will give you (all) rest.' He commands an extraordinary power. Think of sin as a vicious master who harnesses us to a wagon full of lusts, demanding hard service all day, every day. We are made to expend all our energy trying to serve those lusts. Yet they are never satisfied. More is always demanded. Pleasures, honours, and material things are like monsters that, the more they are fed, the bigger and stronger they get. We become 'slaves of sin' (John 8:34; Rom. 6:17; 2 Pet. 2:19). Yet Jesus is able to set us free from this bondage so that it no longer shall have dominion over us (Rom. 6:14, 18).

> He breaks the pow'r of reigning sin,
> He sets the pris'ner free;
> His blood can make the foulest clean,
> His blood availed for me.[3]

His truth sets us free (John 8:32). He liberates us from the guilt of sin, forgiving all our sins, and from the power of sin, breaking its grip on our souls. Do his words resonate? Do I know what soul weariness is? Am I weighed down by guilt? Am I exhausted pulling the wagon-load of lust all day long every day? Am I tired of feeding the monster that continually and increasingly oppresses me? Then I am a candidate to accept the 'Great Invitation.' Jesus welcomes all such to himself. He is 'gentle and humble of heart.' He is gentle with sinners, however twisted they may have been, however vile and corrupt. He promises 'rest for the soul,' rest from

---

[3] Charles Wesley, 'O for a Thousand Tongues to Sing,' in *Trinity Hymnal* (1973; Norcross, GA; Great Commission Publications, 1990), #164, stanza 4.

the guilt, rest from the weariness, rest from the compulsive service of sin, rest from our slavery.

Take my yoke and learn

> *Take my yoke upon you, and learn from me, for I am gentle and lowly in heart, and you will find rest for your souls* (Matt. 11:29).

What is a yoke? A yoke is what hitches an animal to a plough or wagon. It's like a harness. Jesus doesn't unhitch us from our bondage to sin so that we can harness ourselves to a new form of illicit servitude. Rather, he says, 'Take my yoke upon you.' 'Take' is imperative, a command, yet it is still an invitation, and a gracious one at that. We are to unhitch our harness from the wagon of lust and re-hitch it to the wagon of righteousness. By coming to Christ we become slaves of God and of righteousness, which is true freedom (Rom. 6:18-22). What is this yoke? It comes in various forms. There is the yoke of *deprivation*. There are those things which the believer gives up: the lusts of the eyes, of the flesh, and of position and power (1 John 2:15-17). The most cherished sins must be mortified (Rom. 8:13). The yoke of Christ involves loss of sin's passing pleasures (Heb. 11:25), and the scorn and contempt of the world (1 Cor. 4:8-13).

There is the yoke of *affliction*. Jesus promises that his disciples will suffer persecution. They will be hated. They will endure tribulation (John 15:18-25; 16:33). All who desire to live godly in Christ Jesus will be persecuted (2 Tim. 3:12).

Through 'many tribulations' we enter the kingdom of God (Acts 14:22).

There is the yoke of *spiritual discipline*. Believers are sustained as the Holy Spirit takes what Christ has accomplished and applies it to them by the ordinances: the word, sacraments, and prayer, and more broadly, attendance at public services, Sabbath observance, private devotions, and family worship (1 Tim. 4:28). These commitments of thought, time and energy are essential. These yokes are considerable, yet they are *easy* and *light*.

Jesus says, 'Learn from me.' 'Learn,' along with 'Come' and 'Take,' is also an imperative and also a gracious invitation. Learn what? Learn most everything. Learn right from wrong, truth from error, the important from the unimportant, the worthy from the unworthy. Learn about personal weaknesses and vulnerabilities and inability. Learn the difference between worldly freedom (which is bondage) and true freedom that Christ secures for us. Learn to establish right priorities and view life from the right perspective. Learn to trust Christ and depend upon his strength. This is true freedom. How so? Because his yoke hitches us to the purpose for which we were made. That is why Jesus can say that his 'yoke is easy' and his 'burden is light.'

For my yoke is easy, and my burden is light (Matt. 11:30).

There is a yoke. Yet it is an 'easy' yoke. There is a burden. Yet it is a 'light' burden. As we are harnessed to Christ and with him our design for our lives as image-bearers, we find rest for our souls.

How does Jesus impart this rest? We repeat. By offering atonement for our sins through his death. He provides for us forgiveness and the removal of the guilt of our sins. Power flows from the cross freeing us from the power of sin. He cleanses the conscience. He restores us to our Father. He liberates the soul from the yoke of this sinful world. He transforms our nature, recreating us in his own image (2 Cor. 5:17). He imparts his Holy Spirit who indwells and empowers us to live wisely, lovingly, and obediently (e.g. Rom. 8:13).

Resonates

As I've aged, I have developed a passion for Mozart's piano and wind concertos. I listen to them as I study, particularly when reducing my sermon to an outline on Friday mornings in anticipation of preaching on Sunday mornings. They are profoundly beautiful and moving. Now they resonate, whereas when I was younger they did not. Similarly, I once read past John 6:35, 'I am the bread of life,' etc. whereas today I find Jesus' words to be as profound as anything ever spoken.

I quote Matthew 11:28-30 at every communion service as I serve the cup to the elders and conclude the distribution of the elements. Each time I do I am emotionally moved. Jesus is welcoming us to himself. Follow the pronouns.

'Come to *me*,' he says. '*I* will give you rest.' "Take *my* yoke.' 'Learn of *me*.' '*I* am gentle and humble of heart.' '*My* yoke is easy, and *my* burden is light' (KJV). We are invited to him, to a person, not a power, to a relationship, not a religion. Christianity is a religion but that is not primary. Jesus himself offers *his* help to all who will accept it, help that meets all of our fundamental needs. He says, 'Let not your heart be troubled' (John 14:1). He says, 'My peace I give to you' (John 14:27). Believers enjoy a peace that is 'not as the world gives' (John 14:27), a 'peace that passes understanding' (Phil. 4:7). His promise is that his joy will be in us, 'and that our joy may be full' (John 15:11). Believers are enabled to 'rejoice in the Lord always' (Phil. 4:4) and experience 'a joy inexpressible and filled with glory' (1 Pet. 1:8). Believers enjoy contentment 'in any and every circumstance' (Phil. 4:12). How could one possibly reject such a gracious offer? How could one possibly refuse an opportunity so kindly extended? He who spoke these words is one who can be trusted, one to whom we can 'hitch our wagons' and trust for the good of our souls.

5

The Incomparable Christ:
His Teaching

MATTHEW 6:25-34

*Therefore I tell you, do not be anxious about your life,
what you will eat or what you will drink, nor about
your body, what you will put on. Is not life more than
food, and the body more than clothing? Look at the
birds of the air: they neither sow nor reap nor gather
into barns, and yet your heavenly Father feeds them.
Are you not of more value than they? And which of you
by being anxious can add a single hour to his span of
life? And why are you anxious about clothing? Consider
the lilies of the field, how they grow: they neither toil
nor spin, yet I tell you, even Solomon in all his glory
was not arrayed like one of these. But if God so clothes
the grass of the field, which today is alive and tomorrow
is thrown into the oven, will he not much more clothe
you, O you of little faith? Therefore do not be anxious,
saying, 'What shall we eat?' or 'What shall we drink?'
or 'What shall we wear?' For the Gentiles seek after all*

> *these things, and your heavenly Father knows that you*
> *need them all. But seek first the kingdom of God and*
> *his righteousness, and all these things will be added to*
> *you. Therefore do not be anxious about tomorrow, for*
> *tomorrow will be anxious for itself. Sufficient for the*
> *day is its own trouble.*

I HAVE mentioned that I was converted at the age of nine and was baptized at fourteen. I confessed Jesus Christ as Saviour and Lord at the time of those two milestones; never was there a time (that I am able to recall) when my faith did not extend the full length of my knowledge. As far as I am aware, I always believed. I don't recall unbelief ever.

Yet my faith lacked a certain personal element. The inspiration of Matthew 11:28-30 described in the previous chapter did not come during my childhood or early teens. By that I mean that I had not yet been inspired by the life and ministry of Jesus. I had been moved to repent and believe, but not motivated to love and serve. It is difficult to put into words precisely what was missing. My faith lacked the elements of enthusiasm, admiration, conviction, and comfort. That changed along with many other things during my college years. My sophomore year I began to read Matthew's Gospel. I had read it before. I read the Living Bible version of the New Testament in high school. I recall being confused once I arrived halfway through Mark's Gospel, thinking that much of what I was reading I had seen before, which of course I had, reading Matthew, with which Mark shares so much common material. This time it was different, particularly as I began reading the Sermon on the Mount, Matthew 5–7. Let me use an over-worked word. I was *amazed*. One passage in particular hit me with life-changing power, Matthew 6:25-34. There also were several additional passages from the Sermon on the Mount that absolutely captivated and consequently transformed my Christian experience. We will look briefly at these passages and then at several passages from elsewhere, attempting to understand the power of the impact of Jesus's teaching.

Perceptive about religion

Jesus spoke with unparalleled insight about life and religion, about God and man, about time and eternity.

Priorities in life

As a young college student, I struggled with what should be my priority for life. To what should I devote my life? What should be my aim? To what should I channel my time and energy and resources? Then I read Matthew 6:25-34. Jesus' words utterly gripped my soul. Instantly I could see that his words were divine words, words straight from heaven. His words were unparalleled in their power, unequalled in their insight. The key to the passage is in verse 33: 'But seek first the kingdom of God and his righteousness, and all these things will be added to you.' What is to be my priority in life? Jesus tells us. Above all, in all, and behind all that I do, I am to seek first the kingdom of God. Perhaps I will become a teacher. Or perhaps a lawyer. Or maybe a businessman. Regardless, I am in everything from vocation to vacation to seek first God's kingdom and his righteousness. That is clarifying, is it not? Life is all about seeking to know, love, obey, and serve God.

How am I to do this when so much of my mental and physical energy is taken up with the things of life? That is where Jesus' remarkable teaching on trusting our Father in heaven comes in, teaching that I found to be utterly riveting. Listen as he teaches us about trust:

> *Therefore I tell you, do not be anxious about your life, what you will eat or what you will drink, nor about your body, what you will put on. Is not life more than food, and the body more than clothing?* (Matt. 6:25).

Jesus identified exactly what I was anxious about. Food and clothing represent the necessities of life. I was anxious about the future, about where I would work, where I would live, whom I should marry, and how I would make enough money. Jesus understands my concerns. Jesus understands the challenges I face and he is addressing them.

> *Look at the birds of the air: they neither sow nor reap nor gather into barns, and yet your heavenly Father feeds them. Are you not of more value than they? And which of you by being anxious can add a single hour to his span of life? And*

why are you anxious about clothing? Consider the lilies of the field, how they grow: they neither toil nor spin, yet I tell you, even Solomon in all his glory was not arrayed like one of these. But if God so clothes the grass of the field, which today is alive and tomorrow is thrown into the oven, will he not much more clothe you, O you of little faith? (Matt. 6:26-30).

Above all I found Jesus' teaching in verses 26-30 to be utterly compelling. Still to this day I fail to see how anyone can remain untouched by these words. On the one hand, they are beautiful, moving, inspiring words, having almost a poetic quality about them. On the other hand, they were for me convincing, inspiring, and life-changing. 'Even Solomon in all his glory was not arrayed like one of these' (verse 29). And the point: 'will he not much more clothe you, O you of little faith?' (verse 30). These are words upon which one could build one's life. These are life-transforming words. These are life-reorienting words. They are self-authenticatingly divine. Only one who is both God and man could speak such words. 'Never did a man speak as he did,' his contemporaries exclaimed (John 7:46). His voice is the voice of God. His truth is absolute truth. 'The multitudes were amazed at his teaching' (Matt. 7:28).

Trusting in the Father in heaven is the key to establishing the central priority in life: 'Seek first the kingdom of God.' With God's help we can do this. Why? Because we can trust a God who so carefully feeds unimportant birds and so unfailingly clothes worthless 'lilies of the field.' Because our Father in heaven knows our needs (verse 32) and so tenderly and persistently cares for that which is of little value, we can make his kingdom our focus. We can safely be devoted to his kingdom because he will provide 'all these (basic and necessary) things.' They will be 'added to us.' I am free to take risks for the sake of Christ's gospel kingdom. I can go into the ministry or go on the mission field. I can risk rejection as a religious fanatic on campus or in the fraternity house. I can risk tithing my money. I can risk showing radical hospitality. Jesus' words inspired the whole direction of my life.

Motive in life

We mustn't stop merely with priorities. Jesus takes us deeper, to the motives behind the priorities.

> *You are the salt of the earth, but if salt has lost its taste, how shall its saltiness be restored? It is no longer good for anything except to be thrown out and trampled under people's feet. You are the light of the world. A city set on a hill cannot be hidden. Nor do people light a lamp and put it under a basket, but on a stand, and it gives light to all in the house. In the same way, let your light shine before others, so that they may see your good works and give glory to your Father who is in heaven* (Matt. 5:13-16).

Jesus' words moved me. I am to be as salt, preserving and enriching life on earth. I am to be as light, illuminating truth and displaying holiness (both of which light represents). My religious and moral light is to dispel the darkness. Why? So that others might 'see our good works.' Why? So that they might 'give glory to our Father who is in heaven.' What is to be our motive in life? It is to glorify God. This motive is to lie behind all that we are to do. This is the deeper aim behind our priority of kingdom-seeking.

This truth came home to me with heightened clarity in the summer of 1975 when John MacArthur preached at the Grace Brethren Church of Long Beach, California, on 'the glory of God.' His powerful sermon summed it all up. Glorify God is what I want to do. I want to see God get the glory that is his due. I am grieved to see him get anything less. MacArthur cited the *Westminster Shorter Catechism's* first question, which I had never before heard:

> Man's chief end is to glorify God, and to enjoy him forever.

Our goal in life is nothing so unworthy as our own honour, our own prestige, our own glory, but God's. This is a power-ful challenge from Jesus, an illuminating challenge, an inspiring challenge, a direction-setting course of life, and a life-determining insight. This same truth can be expressed from a different angle. Jesus went on to teach us that we are not to sound our trumpet when we give to charitable causes, or stand on street corners when we pray, or put on a gloomy face when we fast. Those who do such things have corrupt motives. Jesus warns,

> *Beware of practising your righteousness before other people*
> *in order to be seen by them, for then you will have no reward*
> *from your Father who is in heaven* (Matt. 6:1).

The motive of religious hypocrites in their religious disciplines is to be 'praised by others' and 'seen by others' (6:2, 5, 16). Their religious service is worthless because their ultimate goal or aim is misplaced. Why should one give, pray, fast, attend church, or engage in any form of religious service? In order to please God! Life is all about pleasing God, not winning the approval of others. This is our 'aim' or 'ambition' (2 Cor. 5:9, NASB). This is what we want to do. This is our goal, our aim, our desire, nothing more, nothing less, whether we speak of glorifying or pleasing God.

It should be clear at this point that reading the Sermon on the Mount brought life-altering clarity to me. Let me remind us of more of what is packed into this the greatest of all sermons:

- The Beatitudes, the ideal virtues (Matt. 5:3-12);
- His exposition of the law of God, particularly its internal application (Matt. 5:21-48);
- The Lord's Prayer, the model prayer (Matt. 6:9-13);
- The Parable of Foundations, whether sand or rock (Matt. 7:24-27).

He insisted that we

- Turn the other cheek, give the coat off our backs, and walk the extra mile (Matt. 5:39-41);

- Love our neighbours and our enemies (Matt. 5:44, 45);
- Judge not lest we be judged (Matt. 7:1);
- Observe the golden rule (Matt. 7:12).

Jesus said these things with such power and such insight, such perception that I knew that I must live for him. I believe in him. I trust him. He is reliable. He is dependable. When he said,

> Come to me, all who labour and are heavy laden, and I will give you rest. Take my yoke upon you, and learn from me, for I am gentle and lowly in heart, and you will find rest for your souls. For my yoke is easy, and my burden is light (Matt. 11:28-30),

I could not but respond and follow unconditionally. Do you feel the power of his invitation? Are his words not compelling? Are you not also moved to respond in complete surrender?

Perceptive about the human condition

The other category of teaching that overwhelmed me was Jesus' insight into the human condition. An early Chinese convert was reported to say upon hearing the Gospels read, 'The one who said those words made my heart.' This was exactly my sense of things.

Parables[1]

We can turn to the parables, Jesus' brilliant, illuminating, inspiring parables, to see what I mean. We may start with the Parable of the Rich Fool (Luke 12:16-21). Here is a man who is a success in this world. He has so much stuff that he has to build bigger barns in which to store it all. This for him is what life is all about. This is what he lives for, what we live for, if left to our own inclinations. We want the stuff of this world. We pursue wealth, things, honours, powers, prestige, fame, yet we never have enough. These things fail to satisfy us. The 'rich fool' thinks he is in control of his destiny. He thinks he has many years before him in which to enjoy his things. 'And I will say to my soul, "Soul, you have ample goods laid up for many years; relax, eat, drink, be merry"' (Luke 12:19). This is how we think. I have 'many years,' he says. Now I can enjoy life. What remarkable insight Jesus shows into our outlook. God says to him, 'Thou fool' (KJV). How powerfully he exposes our foolishness: 'But God said to him, "Fool! This night your soul is required of you, and the things you have prepared, whose will they be?"' (Luke 12:20). Don't you know, rich fool, that you can't take your things with you into the grave? Don't you understand that this life is but preparation for the next? Don't you realize that life is short and eternity is long? Why

---

[1] The present author has written a book entitled *The Parables of Jesus: Entering, Growing, Living and Finishing in God's Kingdom* (Fearn, Ross-shire: Christian Focus Publications, 2010).

then are you living entirely in service of the immediate, the now, the temporal? Why are you working to accumulate that which will not last? Why are you rich towards yourself and not 'rich towards God' (Luke 12:22)? How clarifying is the teaching of Jesus about the withering grass and fading flower of human existence over against the word of God that endures forever (Isa. 40:6-8). Jesus warns, 'Do not work for the food that perishes, but for the food that endures to eternal life' (John 6:27). Don't waste your life. Don't devote your life to that which is perishing. 'Heaven and earth will pass away,' Jesus assures us, 'but my words will not pass away' (Matt. 24:35). Does this parable not place life in its proper perspective? Having challenged us to follow him along the path of self-denial, Jesus asks us again, 'For what will it profit a man if he gains the whole world and forfeits his soul? Or what shall a man give in return for his soul?' (Matt. 16:26). Have the issues of time and eternity ever been expressed with greater clarity? Have they ever been brought into sharper focus?

Jesus' words were decisive for me. No sacrifice is too great in the service of eternity. No price is too high to pay.

The Parable of the Prodigal Son (Luke 15:11-32) is another of these penetrating, insightful passages. The story is well known. We easily identify with one of the sons of the father, if not both. The younger wants to escape the restrictions of his father and so flees with his inheritance to the 'far country.' He squanders his wealth in 'reckless living' (Luke 15:13).

Jesus describes that within us there is that which wants to rebel, that is drawn to the world's attractions and easily seduced by them. This wayward son consumes all his wealth and ends up where? Among the filth of the pigsty, yearning even to eat the food of swine. This is where sin leads. This is the result. The world promises everything but delivers nothing. Its rewards are superficial and temporary, 'passing pleasures' leaving one empty and destitute. Then there is the elder brother. He is at the other end of sin's spectrum. He has conformed to his father's will, obeying and serving him. Yet he has done so with an undercurrent of bitterness. He is self-righteous and proud, condemning his brother's profligacy: 'this son of yours … has devoured your property with prostitutes.' Yet, he says, exhibiting no understanding of grace, 'you killed the fattened calf for him!' (Luke 16:30). I suppose that most of us are not simply one or the other of these two brothers, but both, swinging back and forth between the two, first one, then the other, depending upon our circumstances. What do we need? A Father in heaven who, when he sees us 'still a long way off,' nevertheless 'feels compassion' and runs to embrace and kiss us (Luke 15:20). We need a Father in heaven who when we say, 'Father, I have sinned against heaven and before you,' clothes us in the 'best robe,' the robe of Christ's righteousness, places a ring on our hand, shoes on our feet, kills the fattened calf, and celebrates our return to the family (verses 22-24). Whether my sins follow the pattern of the younger son or the elder brother, Jesus assures me that I have a Father in heaven who is ready to welcome me. He describes with such precision exactly who we are and exactly what we need. His words resonate with our lived experience.

'I am' declarations

Jesus' profound insight into the human condition is evident repeatedly, yet nowhere more so than in the great 'I am' statements of John's Gospel. What is the human condition? It is that of Augustine's (354–430) restless heart and Blaise Pascal's (1623–62) God-shaped void. All through the centuries the accuracy of Jesus' depiction of the emptiness and neediness of human experience has been recognized.

Bread of life

Do we not all experience a hunger in our souls? Is the sense of emptiness, of futility, of meaninglessness not universal? Jesus says to us all, 'I am the bread of life; whoever comes to me shall not hunger, and whoever believes in me shall never thirst' (John 6:35).

Jesus recognizes the hunger, the thirst within us, our desire for that which will satisfy, that which will fulfil. We try various alternatives: money, power, erotic pleasure, fame, prestige, recognition. However, the world makes promises that it cannot fulfil. It only is able to serve up counterfeits that at best provide only a temporary reprieve. The devil's great deception is that of convincing the world that the

Christian life is dull, dreary, boring. Become a Christian and life will be over. One will be consigned to a colourless world of grey. All the excitement, the fun, the thrills in life, most are led to believe, are to be found apart from God and the restrictions of his commandments. Yet Jesus declares that he and he alone is able truly and permanently to satisfy the hunger and quench the thirst of our souls. He is the source of true and lasting fulfilment.

Light of the world

Do we not long for direction in life? We stumble about, listening to various voices as they disagree as to what truly is important. What is vital? What should be my priorities? To what should I devote my life? By what standards or principles am I to live? It is all so confusing. We are bewildered by the various claims that are made. Jesus understands that. He says to us, 'I am the light of the world. Whoever follows me will not walk in darkness, but will have the light of life' (John 8:12).

The world is a dark place. Light represents both truth and purity. He is the light that we need. His light illumines life, its meaning and purpose. It distinguishes truth from error, right from wrong, and fact from fiction. Those who receive Christ receive this light that is a lamp to our feet and a light to our path (Psa. 119:105). He provides the vital direction that we need to live life in this world and to live it in the light of eternity.

Good Shepherd

Jacob at the end of his life praised the God 'who has been my shepherd all my life long to this day' (Gen. 48:15). This is what we all need: God to shepherd us, to lead and guide us through the fog of life. This is what the Good Shepherd provides for all believers (John 10:11-15).

Do we not need protection and care? We are weak, vulnerable, and foolish. Jesus likens us to sheep and identifies himself as the Good Shepherd. His rod corrects and protects us. His staff directs and guides us (Psa. 23). He declares, 'I am the good shepherd. I know my own and my own know me, just as the Father knows me and I know the Father; and I lay down my life for the sheep' (John 10:14, 15).

He fends off the wolves who would devour our souls (verses 11-13). He keeps us safely in the fold (verses 1-4) and leads us to the green pastures and still waters (verses 9, 10). He provides, he protects, he leads, he cares for his sheep. He imparts a sense of safety, of security in what otherwise is a dangerous world.

Resurrection and life

Finally, do we not long to live beyond the grave? Surely this life is not all there is. Is this not why we build our pyramids and tombs, because we long to live on? Is this not why we place our names on buildings and monuments? Life is meaningless if it terminates at our death. Our relationships are futile if our loved ones who have left this world are never to be seen again. Jesus declares, 'I am the resurrection and the life. Whoever believes in me, though he die, yet shall he live, and everyone who lives and believes in me shall never die. Do you believe this?' (John 11:25, 26).

'Do you believe this?' Yes, we do. What Jesus claims rings true. He is the conqueror and transformer of death. He overcame death by rising from the dead and by so doing transformed it for all who believe. We 'shall never die'! Jesus declares, 'I am the way, the truth, and the life. No one comes to the Father except through me' (John 14:6).

I could go on, but I think my point has been made.

Jesus' descriptions of the human condition resonate with us. They ring true. The sheep hear in his voice that of the Good Shepherd (John 10:16). The sheer power of Jesus' words transformed my Christian life. They proved so insightful, so compelling, so convicting, so inspiring that I wanted nothing more than for others to know these words and the one who spoke them. They were self-authenticating, self-testifying, self-verifying. The one who spoke such words was one whom I could trust and for whom I knew I must live.

6

The Incomparable Christ: His True Humanity (1)

JOHN 11:33-44

When Jesus saw her weeping, and the Jews who had come with her also weeping, he was deeply moved in his spirit and greatly troubled. And he said, 'Where have you laid him?' They said to him, 'Lord, come and see.' Jesus wept. So the Jews said, 'See how he loved him!' But some of them said, 'Could not he who opened the eyes of the blind man also have kept this man from dying?' Then Jesus, deeply moved again, came to the tomb. It was a cave, and a stone lay against it. Jesus said, 'Take away the stone.' Martha, the sister of the dead man, said to him, 'Lord, by this time there will be an odour, for he has been dead four days.' Jesus said to her, 'Did I not tell you that if you believed you would see the glory of God?' So they took away the stone. And Jesus lifted up his eyes and said, 'Father, I thank you that you have heard me. I knew that you always hear me, but I said this on account of the people standing around, that they may

> *believe that you sent me.' When he had said these things,*
> *he cried out with a loud voice, 'Lazarus, come out.' The*
> *man who had died came out, his hands and feet bound*
> *with linen strips, and his face wrapped with a cloth.*
> *Jesus said to them, 'Unbind him, and let him go.'*

SOME modern historians have referred to Robert E. Lee, and to a lesser extent George Washington, as 'marble men.' Their image over time, carefully cultivated by earlier historians and biographers, had become that of wise, virtuous, courageous men, near-perfect men, dispassionate men, and therefore barely human men. They seemed never to have been foolish or excessive or self-indulgent, or petty, or angry. They seemed to be of another species. Of course, this portrait was itself deeply flawed as both men had their own feet of clay, which more recent historians have been all too eager to document.

As a young Christian, this was a problem for me in connection with Jesus. His perfections, as I understood them, rendered him remote. In many ways it was easier to relate to the apostle Paul than to Jesus. The apostle becomes so passionate when writing to the Corinthians, Philippians, and Galatians. His frustration, exasperation, and injured feelings are all palpable. He seemed more human than Jesus. It was not until I was in England studying theology that I discovered my misperception. I was assigned to read an article of B. B. Warfield (1851–1921) first published in 1912 entitled, 'On the Emotional Life of Our Lord.'[1] From that point forward my understanding of the humanity of Jesus was revolutionized.

A recurring problem in the history of the church is that of allowing Christ's humanity to consume his divinity or for his divinity to consume his humanity. His humanity is so emphasized by some that his divinity is lost and he is reduced to a weak, pathetic, helpless fellow sufferer who can sympathize but lacks the power or capacity to save. Or his divinity is so emphasized that his humanity is lost, and he appears to us as a detached, aloof, unfeeling Redeemer who has the power to save but cannot sympathize, and so, perhaps seems to lack the inclination to save. What particularly moved me was Warfield's exposition of John 11:33-44. We see there the whole Christ who groans with us in our suffering and who exercises a divine power by which he is able to conquer death.

The divinity of Christ was never a problem for me. I was reared in orthodox Protestant churches which affirmed the Nicene Creed ('truly God and truly man, begotten not made, being of one substance with the Father'), and the Chalcedonian formula (the human and divine natures are united, yet 'without confusion, without change, without division, without separation'). It was not the divinity but the fullness of Christ's humanity that had eluded me.

---

[1] B. B. Warfield, 'On the Emotional Life of Our Lord,' *The Person and Work of Christ* (Philadelphia: Presbyterian & Reformed Publishers, 1950).

The current passage more than any other helped me to understand the reality of Christ's human emotional life. After examining Jesus' response to death, we will go back to review the Gospels to discover what perhaps in the past we have read over too quickly; that is, we will re-examine their rich portrait of Jesus' very human emotional life.

Case study: Jesus responding to death

The apostle John describes a two-fold response by Jesus to the weeping of Mary and her comforters on the occasion of the tragedy of Lazarus' death.

> *When Jesus saw her weeping, and the Jews who had come with her also weeping, he was deeply moved in his spirit and greatly troubled* (John 11:33).

This is a very human scene like that which has been repeated countless times throughout the centuries. A loved one dies prematurely or unexpectedly. Those left behind are devastated by the loss, grieving their absence, and questioning God's timing or failure to act (see John 11:21, 32). Jesus enters the scene. How does he respond?

Troubled

First, Jesus was troubled. 'Jesus saw (Mary) weeping' and was emotionally moved. Two verbs describe this initial response. The first verb, translated 'deeply moved in his spirit' (*embrimaomai* plus *tō pneumati*) or 'groaned in his spirit' (KJV, NKJV), is used in extra-biblical Greek for the snorting of horses, and when applied to humans, indicates suppressed anger, outrage, or indignation (cf. Mark 14:4, 5).[2] It indicates not mere disapproval of the surrounding commotion, but 'irrepressible anger,' says Warfield again, even 'just rage.'[3] 'In the spirit' indicates in Jesus' innermost being, 'with heart swelling with indignation at the outrage of death.'[4] He rages at the sin, sickness, grief, and death, what Job calls 'the king of terrors,' that stalks this fallen world (Job 18:14).

A second verb translated 'greatly troubled' (*trassō*, plus *heauton*, lit. 'troubled himself'), or 'deeply troubled' also indicates, Warfield argues, 'a profound agitation of his whole being.'[5] It is used of the stirring up of the water at Bethesda (John 5:7). 'He shook with emotion.'[6] At what then was he disturbed? He is at a graveside. A friend has died. Loved ones are weeping. He is disturbed, troubled by the tragedy of death. He is moved by 'the common misery of the human

---

[2] Perhaps indicating 'a groan of indignation from his innermost being' (Zerwick, Max and Mary Grosvenor, *A Grammatical Analysis of the Greek New Testament*, Vol. 1 [Rome: Biblical Institute Press, 1974], I:321). See also George Hutcheson, *The Gospel of John, Geneva Series Commentary* (1657, 1841; repr. London: Banner of Truth Trust, 1972), 231; Alfred Plummer: 'It expresses not sorrow but *indignation* or severity' (*The Gospel According to John, Cambridge Greek Testament* [Cambridge: University Press, 1929], 242).

[3] Warfield, 'Emotional Life of Our Lord,' 115.

[4] *Ibid.*, 100.

[5] *Ibid.*, 116.

[6] F. F. Bruce, *The Gospel of John: Introduction, Exposition, Notes* (Grand Rapids: William B. Eerdmans Publishing Company, 1974), 246; Plummer: 'He allowed his emotion to become evident by some external movement such as a shudder.' *John*, 243.

race,' says Calvin.[7] Jesus considers 'the woeful effects of sin that brought death into the world,' says the Puritan John Trapp (1601–69), 'and makes them a ghastly and loathsome spectacle.'[8] Warfield speaks of Jesus' profound 'repugnance to death and all that death meant.'[9] We find Jesus similarly 'troubled' as he contemplates the 'hour' of his death (12:27), and again at his imminent betrayal (13:21). 'Jesus,' says Matthew Henry, 'had all the passions and affections of human nature.'[10] This is Jesus' first response.

Weeping

Second, Jesus quietly wept. 'And he said, "Where have you laid him?" They said to him, "Lord, come and see." Jesus wept' (John 11:34, 35).

The second response of Jesus is that of quiet weeping. Why does he weep? Different words are used for the weeping of Mary and the crowd (loud, unrestrained weeping,

---

[7] Calvin, *John*, II:11.

[8] Trapp, *Commentary*, V:384; Hutcheson: Jesus' indignation was directed 'chiefly against sin and Satan, that brought all this misery' (*John*, 231); Bruce: 'It was the presence of sickness and death, and the havoc they wrought in human life' (246). Lightfoot says of verse 33, 'The expression ("was troubled" or "greatly troubled") is a way of showing that Jesus of his own free will entered fully into man's lot, identifying himself with the griefs of his friends' (in Leon Morris, *The Gospel According to John, The New International Commentary on the New Testament*, Grand Rapids: Wm. B. Eerdmans Pub. Co., 1971, 557, n. 69).

[9] Warfield, 'Emotional Life of Our Lord,' 129.

[10] Henry, *Exposition*, on John 11:33-35.

wailing, verses 31 and 33), and that of Jesus (quiet tears).[11] His tears are tears of sympathy. He weeps because of the suffering of his friend Lazarus and the emotional pain of his sisters. He was moved by the tears of others, just as we are. When D. A. Carson claims, 'It is unreasonable to think that Jesus' tears were shed for Lazarus, since he knew he was about to raise him from the dead,' he misses the point entirely.[12] The natural human response to the sorrow of others is to weep along with them.

Let me provide a poignant example. In December of 2011, most of the membership of Christ Episcopal Church of Savannah enjoyed their last service in their historic building and walked together several blocks to the Independent Presbyterian Church. Their three hundred were greeted by five hundred of our members welcoming them to the use of our buildings which we would share while they were 'homeless.' As they arrived, many of them were weeping. Before long, our people were weeping along with them. This is a common human response. Even fictional weeping on the silver screen, even cartoon, fictional sadness and weeping evokes our empathetic tears. Our entire family gathered in a parking lot after seeing *Toy Story 3*, crying together for the passing of our children's childhood and of our family life that would never again be as it was.

---

[11] *Klaiō*, wailing, *dakruō*, quiet weeping.
[12] D. A. Carson, *The Gospel According to John* (Grand Rapids, MI: Wm. B. Eerdmans Publishing Co., 1991), 412.

Jesus is not an automaton, but a real man. Jesus grieves for the experience of death that Lazarus endured, and for the suffering of the loved ones and family. Think of all that death means. It tears the soul from the body, an unnatural act that by instinct and nature we abhor. It robs us of our loved ones, who cross a gulf that is unbridgeable and absolute. It is God's judgment upon Adam and Eve and all of their descendants. It is the source of untold pain, sorrow, grief, and sadness. So Jesus both rages and weeps. 'He shows by his groaning "spirit,"' says Calvin, 'a strong emotion and by tears, that he is as much affected by our ills *as if he had suffered them in himself.*' 'He who later shared the pains of death here shares the sorrow for death,' says Alfred Plummer (1841–1926).[13] 'He wept out of compassion for all humanity, which is subject to death,' says the ancient church father Cyril of Alexandria (375–444).[14]

Jesus is not a cold, stoic Saviour. He fulfills his own command to 'weep with those who weep' (Rom. 12:15). David Brown speaks of 'the sublime spectacle of *the Son of God* in tears.'[15] Campbell Morgan (1863–1945), the popular London preacher, calls it 'a most remarkable unveiling of the heart of Jesus.'[16] 'It may make trouble sweet to us,' George Hutcheson (1626–74) urges, 'considering that we have such a sympathizer.'[17]

[13] Plummer, *John*, 243.
[14] Cited in *ACCS*, 22.
[15] Brown, *Four Gospels*, 419.
[16] In Morris, *John*, 557, note 69.
[17] Hutcheson, *John*, 231.

His weeping was not an infrequent occurrence. The writer to the Hebrews tells us that, 'In the days of his flesh, Jesus offered up prayers and supplications, with loud cries and tears, to him who was able to save him from death, and he was heard because of his reverence' (Heb. 5:7). Recall Jesus weeping over Jerusalem's unbelief (Luke 19:41). Jesus groans with us in the pain we suffer in a fallen world. 'For we do not have a high priest who cannot sympathize with our weaknesses,' says the writer to the Hebrews, 'but one who has been tempted in all things as we are, yet without sin' (Heb. 4:15). 'He was like us in the emotions of the soul,' says Calvin again.[18] 'He weeps,' says Warfield, 'in true sympathy with the grief of which he was witness.'[19] Jesus not only shed tears for us, Trapp maintains, but also shed '*the dearest and warmest blood in all his heart.*'[20] This is why those mourners of Lazarus visiting from Jerusalem (John 11:18, 31) respond as they do: 'So the Jews said, "See how he loved him!"' (John 11:36). 'We thank you, O ye visitors from Jerusalem, for this spontaneous testimony to the *human softness* of the Son of God,' Brown exclaims.[21] Jesus doesn't respond to our suffering with a shrug.

Years ago, I was in a particularly tough spot. People were aggressively and publicly attacking my ministry and family.

[18] Calvin, *John*, II:12 (emphasis added).
[19] Warfield, 'Emotional Life of Our Lord,' 116.
[20] Trapp, *Commentary*, V:384.
[21] Brown, *Four Gospels*, 419; Henry adds, 'Though our tears profit not the dead, they embalm their memory' (*Exposition*, on John 11:35).

My wife Emily and I went down the street to get counsel from the Rev. William Ralston (*d.* 2003) of St John's Episcopal Church. I explained the whole situation. Emily cried. How did Ralston respond? With deep sympathy. Was that all? No. He cursed them. He shouldn't have, but he did. He was angered. Somehow it was terribly comforting that he both sympathized with us and was angered by the evil. Jesus' response is a mixture of sympathetic grief to the loss that death inflicts and rage against death itself, death the oppressor, death the tyrant, death the reminder of the creature's rebellion against the Creator.

Consequently, Jesus approaches the tomb of Lazarus not merely with tears, but like a warrior to subdue an enemy. 'Christ does not come to the sepulchre as an idle spectator,' says Calvin, 'but like a wrestler preparing for the contest.'[22] Not only does Jesus sympathize, but he attacks the citadel of death. He orders that the tomb be opened: 'Then Jesus, deeply moved again, came to the tomb. It was a cave, and a stone lay against it. Jesus said, 'Take away the stone' (John 11:38, 39).

Jesus was 'deeply moved' or 'groaning in himself' (KJV, NKJV), we are told a second time (11:33), 'for the violent tyranny of death,' says Calvin.[23] His rage is renewed at the sight of the grave. His response further demonstrates Jesus 'to be truly man, and not without human affections,' says

---

[22] Calvin, *John*, II:13.
[23] *Ibid.*.

another Puritan commentator, Matthew Poole (1624–79).[24] He groaned, says Henry, 'as one that would affect himself with the calamitous state of human nature.'[25]

Why this range of emotion in response to the death of Lazarus, from weeping to disturbed to anger? Because death is the wages of sin (Rom. 6:23). Sin is not a thing of indifference. Sin is at the root of all that is harmful and hurtful in this life. Sin, defined as violations of the laws of God, always is destructive. It always is harmful. All human suffering, all human pain, all human heartbreak, all sadness, all weeping, all mourning is a product of sin, going back to Adam's sin, resulting in a fallen world, and our own personal sin. Sin is not glamorous. Sin is not exciting, though a lot of money can be made by portraying it as such. The tomb represents all of this and the sight of it renews Jesus' indignation. His compassion, his grief and anger are not a passing thing.

Warfield beautifully summarizes the whole scene:

> The spectacle of the distress of Mary and her companions enraged Jesus because it brought poignantly home to his consciousness the evil of death, its unnaturalness, its 'violent tyranny' as Calvin (on verse 38) phrases it. In Mary's grief, he 'contemplates'—still to adopt Calvin's words (on verse 33),—'the general misery of the whole human race' and burns with rage against the oppressor of men. Inextinguishable fury seizes upon him; his whole

[24] Poole, *Commentary*, III:340; Chrysostom: 'that you may learn that he had truly put on our nature' (*ACCS*, 4b:20).

[25] Henry, *Exposition*, on John 11:38.

being is discomposed and perturbed; and his heart, if not his lips, cries out,—

> For the innumerable dead
> Is my soul disquieted.

It is death that is the object of his wrath, and behind death him who has the power of death, and whom he has come into the world to destroy. Tears of sympathy may fill his eyes, but this is incidental. His soul is held by rage: and he advances to the tomb, in Calvin's words again, 'as a champion who prepares for conflict.' The raising of Lazarus thus becomes, not an isolated marvel, but—as indeed it is presented throughout the whole narrative (compare especially, verses 24-26)—a decisive instance and open symbol of Jesus' conquest of death and hell. What John does for us in this particular statement is to uncover to us the heart of Jesus, as he wins for us our salvation. Not in cold unconcern, but in flaming wrath against the foe, Jesus smites in our behalf. He has not only saved us from the evils which oppress us; he has felt for and with us in our oppression, and under the impulse of these feelings has wrought out our redemption.[26]

Smite death he does on our behalf. He prays to the Father and then cries out with a loud voice, 'Lazarus, come out,' with the result, John tells us, 'The man who had died came out, his hands and feet bound with linen strips, and

---

[26] Warfield, 'Emotional Life of Our Lord,' 116-117.

his face wrapped with a cloth. Jesus said to them, "Unbind him, and let him go"' (John 11:44).

Enraged by sin, evil, and death, weeping for the resulting human suffering and sorrow, Jesus conquers death on our behalf, not empty of feeling, but with deep internal emotion.

Ascended Christ

We may now look more broadly at the Gospel writers' descriptions of Jesus' internal life. Our question may be, is this display of emotion at the tomb of Lazarus a one-off thing? Or do we see it elsewhere? However, before we do so we need to address another question too. Does Jesus now in heaven have the same sympathy for our suffering and militancy toward our enemies as he demonstrated at the tomb of Lazarus? After all, he is now at the right hand of God, 'far above all rule and authority and power and dominion' (Eph. 1:21). Our great 'high priest' has now 'passed through the heavens' (Heb. 4:14). He is now 'highly exalted,' having 'the name that is above every name' (Phil. 2:9). Thomas Goodwin (1600–80), in his classic work *The Heart of Christ*, states what might be our concern: 'having cast off the frailties of his flesh which he had here, and having clothed his human nature with so great a glory,' is it possible that 'he cannot now pity us … nor be so feelingly affected and touched with our miseries, so as to be tenderly moved to compassionate and commiserate us,' because 'his state and condition now is above all such affections.'[27] It would seem that it is precisely to address this concern that the writer to the Hebrews follows 4:14 with 4:15: 'For we do not have a high priest who is unable to sympathize with our weaknesses, but one who in every respect has been tempted as we are, yet without sin.' The short answer is, yes. He is able to sympathize because he remains both human and divine in heaven; he retains his human nature in which he suffered and was tempted.

The double negative, 'we do *not* have a high priest who is *not* able' (unable), equals an especially strong affirmative as we say in English, 'There is *no* way that I will *not* …' Our high priest, though he has 'passed through the heavens,' *is able* to 'sympathize,' a compound word joining 'suffer' and 'with.' He is *able* (*dunamai*, from which we get our word *dynamite*), a word which in connection with sympathy 'imports an inward faculty, a disposition, a heart that knows how to be compassionate,' says Goodwin. It indicates not an 'external power,' he continues, but 'an internal touch in his will; he hath a heart able to forgive and to afford help.'[28]

We are characterized by 'weakness,' a compound word meaning 'without strength.' We are weak, fragile, vulnerable, tempted, and tested. Yet he is able to suffer with us, though he is now in his highly exalted place, because he too has been 'tempted' or 'tested' by all that which afflicts our finite

[27] Thomas Goodwin, *The Heart of Christ* (1651; repr. Edinburgh: Banner of Truth Trust, 2011), 51.

[28] Goodwin, *Heart of Christ*, 98.

humanity. He has been tempted '*in every respect … as we are,*' or literally, 'according to our likeness,' excepting sin. The writer to the Hebrews goes on to describe the qualifications of a high priest, the point of which is to highlight how Christ meets those qualifications: 'He can deal gently with the ignorant and wayward, since he himself is beset with weakness' (Heb. 5:2). As a high priest he is one who 'can deal gently' or more literally *is able* (again, *dunamai*) to 'have *compassion*' (Heb. 5:2 KJV, *metriopatheō*), a word, says Goodwin, that is 'exceeding emphatical.' It combines *metrios*, to measure, with *pathein*, to suffer with. This measured or moderated sympathy is extended both to the 'ignorant,' those who sin without knowledge, and the 'wayward,' those who sin deliberately and characteristically. These are the two ends of the sin-spectrum which carry along with them all manner of sin that lies between these poles. Towards the whole range of sinners he responds with compassion, with sympathy, as measured by the greatness of the need. It indicates, says Goodwin, that Christ 'can have compassion according to the measure of every one's distress … that (he) considers every circumstance in it, and will accordingly offer his pity and help … and hath a great fellow feeling of it.'[29] It is in his nature to identity with our weakness and to sympathize with us and thus to act from heaven on our behalf: 'Let us then with confidence draw near to the throne of grace, that we may receive mercy and find grace to help in time of need' (Heb. 4:16).

[29] Goodwin, *Heart of Christ*, 137.

We are able to 'draw near' in prayer to God's throne in heaven 'with confidence' or even 'boldly,' knowing that we will receive 'mercy' in connection with our suffering (the special concern of mercy) and 'grace' in connection with weakness, particularly in dealing with temptations to sin, 'to help in time of need' (cf. Heb. 2:17, 18). 'Thy misery can never exceed his mercy,' says Goodwin.[30] Given what repeatedly we see of the depth of Jesus' human emotions in the Gospel record, and given the continuity between his outlook then and his outlook now in heaven, we can be confident that he continues to love us, *compassionately* to sympathize with us and *militantly* to defend us.

[30] Goodwin, *Heart of Christ*, 99.

7

The Incomparable Christ: His True Humanity (2)

JOHN 11:33-44

WE have established that the emotional outlook and conse-
quent actions of Jesus on our behalf are the same now as
they were in his earthly ministry. Now that he is 'highly
exalted' and his humanity is glorified, it is a true humanity,
a thoroughly tested and tempted humanity. We may again
cite the writer to the Hebrews,

> *Therefore he had to be made like his brothers in every respect,
> so that he might become a merciful and faithful high priest
> in the service of God, to make propitiation for the sins of the
> people. For because he himself has suffered when tempted, he
> is able to help those who are being tempted* (Heb. 2:17, 18).

He is a 'merciful' high priest because he himself has
'suffered when tempted.' He has experienced the suffering
that we experience. He is a 'faithful' high priest in that he
has dealt with our sins, having made 'propitiation' and so

can be counted upon, relied upon 'to help.' He is not aloof, emotionally distant, or remote. He is not without under- standing or sympathy. As is repeated in Hebrews 4:15, he was 'made like (us) in every respect,' sharing all our finite weakness and limitations and so 'he is able to help.' He not only is *able* to be faithful but he is *able* to be merciful. This indicates a state of mind, a capacity, an outlook. He is inclined, even eager to show mercy and to come to our aid.

Emotional Portrait

We are now ready to move beyond our 'case study' in Jesus' internal life, seen in his response to the death of Lazarus (John 11:33, 34), his rage against evil and his tears of sympathy for human suffering. What is the full emotional picture of Christ that the gospel writers paint for us? Do we find deep emotions elsewhere? What does his internal life look like across the gospel record?

Compassion

First, we see Jesus responding to suffering and ignorance with *compassion*.[1] The root meaning of the term behind our English word is rare outside of the New Testament, referring to the churning of internal organs in response to sadness, what we colloquially call a 'gut punch.' It is the strongest word for pity in the Greek language. It indicates a strong physiological reaction to suffering. Jesus is moved by

---

[1] Greek *splagchnizomai*.

sympathy *within* and benevolent action *without* in response. He looks sympathetically on the suffering of others and responds with compassion.

Compassion is the emotion most frequently attributed to Jesus. When Jesus looks out at the crowds of people, uninformed, confused, exploited, neglected, how does he respond? Is he contemptuous? Is he condescending? Does he see them as the great unwashed? No, Matthew tells us,

> *When he saw the crowds, he had compassion for them, because they were harassed and helpless, like sheep without a shepherd* (Matt. 9:36; cf. Mark 6:34).

Mark adds,

> *He began to teach them many things* (Mark 6:34).

Whom does Jesus see? The *crowds*. The ordinary people. These are not the highly esteemed priestly caste or the religiously observant Pharisees, or the politically powerful Sadducees and Herodians. These are victims, manipulated and exploited by the political and religious elites. These are the 'harassed and helpless.' Like 'sheep without a shepherd,' these are the defenceless and directionless, neglected and forgotten, wandering about aimlessly, vulnerable to predators and the natural elements. Does Jesus despise their weakness? No, he addresses the spiritual destitution of the masses, their profound ignorance and confusion, by teaching them. Teaching is the rod by which he will protect them from thieves and robbers and wolves (John 10:10-15).

Teaching is the staff by which he will lead and guide them to green pastures and still waters, and most importantly, into the paths of righteousness (Psa. 23:2, 3; John 10:1, 9). He is a *light* to those in the darkness of ignorance (John 12:35). He is the *way* for wandering and lost sheep. He is the *truth* for those neglected and exploited (14:6).

A second time he looks out at the crowd and sees the sick and suffering. How does he respond? Does he regard physical suffering as unimportant? Is he the type of 'holy man' who only cares about 'spiritual' matters and for which all things material are secondary? No, Matthew tells us, 'When he went ashore he saw a great crowd, and he had compassion on them and healed their sick' (Matt. 14:14). He healed the sick. Why? Out of compassion for their suffering. He is not indifferent to human suffering. He is not cold and unmoved by the pain of our afflictions. He views us with sympathy and acts to relieve our suffering.

A third time he looks out at the crowd and perceives their hunger. The disciples are coldly indifferent. They want nothing to do with relieving the suffering of the hungry crowd. Jesus is not content merely to feed them spiritual food even if the spiritual food is the priority. Matthew tells us,

> *Jesus called his disciples to him and said, 'I have compassion on the crowd because they have been with me now three days and have nothing to eat. And I am unwilling to send them away hungry, lest they faint on the way'* (Matt. 15:32; cf. Mark 6:4; 8:2).

How does Jesus respond to end-of-the-day hunger? This is not life-threatening suffering. It is more run-of-the-mill, more ordinary suffering. Yet he responds with compassion. He is concerned that they might 'faint on the way.' He sympathizes with the very outset of human discomfort, the beginning of our pain, even if it is only the recent onset of hunger pain. Jesus responds by multiplying the loaves, feeding the 5,000 men, plus women and children.

His compassion is not merely for the crowd, but for the individual as well. When he encounters the weeping widow of Nain whose only son had died, Jesus singles her out of the great crowd and, Luke tells us, had *compassion* on her: 'And when the Lord saw her, he had compassion on her and said to her, "Do not weep"' (Luke 7:13). 'When the Lord saw her,' saw her in her sad, pathetic, grieving, weeping, destitute condition, his *reflexive emotional response was compassion* and his immediate action was to raise her son from the dead. This is how he responds to our sadness. This is how he responds to our grief. He is moved with *compassion*. 'None of our secret sorrows,' says the Puritan commentator Joseph Hall (*c.* 1575–1635), 'can be hid from thine eyes or *kept from thy heart*.'[2]

Mercy is another term used to refer to Jesus' compassionate response to suffering.[3] When the blind cry for mercy

---

[2] Joseph Hall, *Contemplations on the Historical Passages of the Old and New Testament*, Volumes I-III (1833; repr. Morgan, PA; Soli Deo Gloria, 1995), III:102 (emphasis added).

[3] Greek *eleeō.*

(Matt. 9:27-31; 20:30, 31; Mark 9:47, 48; Luke 18:38-43), when a mother cries for mercy for her demon-possessed daughter (Matt. 15:22), when a father cries for mercy for his demon-possessed son (Matt. 17:5; cf. Mark 5:19), when lepers cry for mercy to be healed (Luke 17:13), he shows mercy by relieving their suffering and meeting their need. This is what he did then and this is what he does today.

Love

The compassion of Jesus that we just surveyed was an outgrowth of his love. Only once in the Synoptic Gospels are we told that Jesus loved—in the case of the rich young ruler (Mark 10:21). Yet in John's Gospel, love is highlighted as the foundational motive behind all of his work. 'Jesus' prime characteristic was love,' says Warfield, 'and love is the foundation of compassion.'[4] John characterizes Jesus' whole mission as being motivated by love. 'Having loved his own who were in the world,' he writes of all that Jesus, who 'was in the beginning with God,' set out to do (John 1:1, 2). 'He loved them to the end,' the *teleos*, to the end of his life and the completion of his mission (John 13:1). Love, says Hutcheson, is 'the sum of his dealing towards his own.'[5] It is, adds J. C. Ryle (1816–1900), 'the very essence and marrow of the gospel.'[6] In a defining statement, Jesus said, 'Greater

---

[4] Warfield, 'The Emotional Life of Our Lord,' 101.

[5] Hutcheson, *John*, 270.

[6] Ryle, *Expository Thoughts on the Gospels: John*, (1873; repr. Edinburgh: Banner of Truth Trust, 2020), III:1.

love has no one than this, that someone lay down his life for his friends' (John 15:13). Jesus laid down his life for his friends. Why? The greatest of love prompted it. Love was behind the cross. Repeatedly Jesus speaks of his love for his disciples:

> By this my Father is glorified, that you bear much fruit and so prove to be my disciples. As the Father has loved me, so have I loved you. Abide in my love. If you keep my commandments, you will abide in my love, just as I have kept my Father's commandments and abide in his love. These things I have spoken to you, that my joy may be in you, and that your joy may be full. This is my commandment, that you love one another as I have loved you (John 15:8-12).

'I loved you … abide in my love … I have loved you.' Jesus presents his love for his people as a present and enduring reality. His love for them is a model for imitation (John 13:34), and the believer's greatest reward (John 14:21).

Warfield argues that sometimes 'love' when attributed to Jesus refers to 'simple human fondness,' as when applied to 'the disciple whom Jesus loved,' meaning John, that one upon whom 'he especially poured out his personal affection' (John 13:27; 19:26; 20:2; 21:7, 20).[7] Again, we are told that Jesus has a special love for Lazarus (John 11:3) and his sisters Mary and Martha. 'Now Jesus loved Martha and her sister and Lazarus' (John 11:5). It is natural and not sinful for us to have special affection for some and not others, such as those

[7] Warfield, 'Emotional Life of Our Lord,' 105.

whom we marry and the children which we share, as well as others to whom we are drawn in close friendships. These close friendships can be corrupted, becoming exclusive, closed, and cliquish, just as any good thing can be corrupted. Yet of themselves they are good, not evil. Jesus experienced distinctive human affection for some over others. While he loved all his disciples, identifying them as family (Matt. 12:50) and 'friends' (John 15:14), 'he had also the companions of his human heart,' says Warfield; 'those to whom his affections turned in a purely human attachment.'[8]

Yet more generally, Christ's love is for all his people without distinction, as we see manifest in its ultimate expression at the cross. As the apostle writes, 'Therefore be imitators of God, as beloved children. And walk in love, as Christ loved us and gave himself up for us, a fragrant offering and sacrifice to God' (Eph. 5:1, 2). How does Jesus look upon me? With *love*. Yes, but I am a sinner. With *love*. Yet I stumble, fall, and fail. With *love*. Christ died for sinners. Our High Priest looks at his flawed children with *love*.

Anger and grief

Anger and grief are closely associated in Jesus' response to evil, as we saw at the tomb of Lazarus. Confronted with Jerusalem's unbelief, Jesus cries out,

> *And when he drew near and saw the city, he wept over it, saying, 'Would that you, even you, had known on this day*

[8] Warfield, 'Emotional Life of Our Lord,' 106.

the things that make for peace! But now they are hidden from your eyes' (Luke 19:41, 42).

He 'wept,' a term that indicates, says Warfield, 'audible wailing.'[9] He 'burst into sobbing,' says the commentator Leon Morris (1914–2006).[10] This contrasts with Jesus' quiet weeping at the tomb.[11] Jesus knows of the city's hostility. He knows what lies ahead in a matter of days for him. He knows of the coming judgment of God. So he weeps. He weeps for fallen, rebellious, mired humanity. He is not indifferent to moral evil. He is no detached observer of human tragedy. The sadness, the tragedy of unbelief, the catastrophe, the stupidity that is evil draws his tears.

When Jesus set about on the Sabbath to heal a man with a withered hand, he asked his critics, '"Is it lawful on the Sabbath to do good or to do harm, to save life or to kill?" But they were silent' (Mark 3:4). Mark tells us that 'he looked around at them with anger, grieved at their hardness of heart, and said to the man, "Stretch out your hand." He stretched it out, and his hand was restored' (Mark 3:5).

We have combined under our current heading 'grief' and 'anger' because so often they are combined in human experience. In the context of culpable tragedy we find

[9] Greek, *klaiō*; Warfield: 'Emotional Life of Our Lord,' 100.
[10] Leon Morris, *The Gospel According to Luke: An Introduction and Commentary*, Tyndale New Testament Commentaries (1974; Downer's Grove: InterVarsity Press, 2007), 280.
[11] Greek, *dakruō*.

ourselves angry because of the foolishness or heartlessness that brought on the tragedy, and saddened by the resulting pain and suffering. Jesus is angered by the harshness, the hardness, even the cruelty of evil. He looked at their hard, compassionless faces with 'anger' (*orgēs*) and was 'grieved' (an intensive form of *lupeō,* to be sad) at what their silence revealed about their hearts. This grief rose up from deep within his soul. He is 'grieved at their hardness of heart.'

Mark tells us that Jesus 'sighed deeply' (an intensive form of the verb *stenazō*) when the Pharisees demanded of him yet another 'sign' (Mark 8:12). When the disciples rebuked those who were 'bringing children to Jesus that he might touch them,' Jesus was 'indignant' (Mark 10:13, 14; Matt. 19:13; Luke 18:15). He became irritated, annoyed, or vexed at his disciples and showed it with his response: 'Let the children come to me; do not hinder them, for to such belongs the kingdom of God' (Mark 10:14).[12] Jesus responds both 'with anger at the spectacle of inhumanity,' says Warfield, as well as 'with irritation at the spectacle of blundering misunderstanding, however well-meant.'[13]

Another way in which Jesus' anger at evil is expressed is by the use of the term 'rebuked' (*epitimaō*) just used above and used in connection with correcting error, calming natural forces, and healing. The term implies displeasure or even

---

[12] 'He showed his annoyance,—whether by gesture or tone or the mere shortness of his speech.' Warfield, 'Emotional Life of Our Lord,' 110.
[13] *Ibid.*

indignant anger as he corrected Peter's presumption (Mark 8:32), the disciples' vengefulness (Luke 9:55), and their unbelief (Mark 16:14, though a different verb this time), as well as when he stilled the wind and the waves (Matt. 8:26; Mark 4:39; Luke 8:24), and healed the afflicted (Luke 4:35) and demon-possessed (Matt. 17:18; Mark 1:25; 9:25; Luke 4:35, 41; 9:42). Whether encountering unbelief, rampaging nature, disease, or demon possession, Jesus was moved by indignant anger to rebuke the evil and rescue its victims. We see him chiding his disciples, banishing the demons that were tormenting men, and controlling the natural forces which were menacing their lives and safety.

Further, we find Jesus cleansing the temple, motivated by a 'zeal' (*zēlos*) that 'consumes' him. It has 'eaten me up' (John 2:17, KJV, NKJV). Jesus uses physical force, taking up a whip and turning over the tables in the face of desecration of the temple and the worship of God. English New Testament scholar B. F. Westcott (1825–1901) described Jesus' zeal as 'burning jealousy for the holiness of the house of God.'[14]

Jesus is willing to assault his evil opponents with severe language. He calls Herod 'that fox' (Luke 12:32). Others he labels 'swine' (Matt. 7:6), Satan (Mark 8:33), hypocrites (repeatedly). He describes his learned and religious enemies as 'blind guides,' 'blind fools,' 'whitewashed tombs,'

---

[14] Cited by Warfield, 'Emotional Life of Our Lord,' 120; Warfield himself describes it as 'hot indignation at the pollution of the house of God' (*Ibid.*).

'serpents,' 'brood of vipers' (Matt. 23:16, 17, 24), 'ravenous wolves' (Matt. 7:15), and children of the devil (John 8:44).

Jesus is that one who is merciful to those who are needy and suffering, and is at the same time severe toward and opposed to the source of their suffering. Mercy without righteous anger is mere tolerance, what others have called 'the vice of insensibility.' Those who are truly merciful are zealous to remove the source of human suffering and angry towards those forces which perpetuate that suffering. 'Jesus' anger is not merely the seamy side of his pity,' says Warfield; 'it is the righteous reaction of his moral sense in the presence of evil.'[15] Jesus is grieved by human suffering, and grieved more deeply still by the evil of obstinate unbelief.

Sadness and distress

Jesus is compassionate towards us in our suffering and angry towards the evil that is the cause behind it. Still I might wonder, does he know what it means to suffer? After all, he is the Son of God. He is almighty. Did he really experience the pain or was he somehow above it all? Was he ultimately untouched by it all? Jesus, we are assured, was 'the man of sorrows and acquainted with grief' (Isa. 53:3). We see this in particular in connection with his death. Here, more than anywhere else, we see his mental suffering emphasized. At the height of his earthly ministry, he cried out, 'I have a baptism to be baptized with, and how great is my distress

[15] *Ibid.*, 122.

until it is accomplished!' (Luke 12:50, cf. Mark 10:38). His *distress* (*sunexomai*) is *great*. He feels the pressure of his coming torments. He anticipates his approaching suffering with 'anguish' of soul (Isa. 53:11). The cross is a thing to be 'endured' and 'despised' (Heb. 12:1, 2). The prospect turns his life into what has been called a 'perpetual Gethsemane.'

A few days before Gethsemane, Jesus exclaimed, 'Now is my soul troubled' (*trassō*), agitated, disturbed, unsettled (as we have seen) by the prospect of the 'hour' of his passion (John 12:27).

'There was a struggle,' says Matthew Henry, 'between the work he had taken upon him, which required sufferings, and the nature he had taken upon him, which dreaded them.'[16] The agitation he experienced at the tomb of Lazarus he experienced with compounded intensity at his eminent death.

At the Garden of Gethsemane Jesus was in 'agony' (*agōnia*, Luke 22:44), which Warfield identifies as 'the anguish of reluctance,' and describes as 'loathing, aversion, perhaps not unmixed with despondency.'[17] Matthew describes Jesus as 'sorrowful (*lupeō*) and troubled (*adēmoneō*)' (Matt. 26:37). Thomas Goodwin, in his work 'Of Christ the Mediator,' understands the second of these terms as meaning 'to be wholly taken and swallowed up with sorrow and amazement

---

[16] Henry, *Exposition*, on John 12:27.
[17] Warfield, 'Emotional Life of Our Lord,' 130.

… and to forget all comfort whatsoever.'[18] Matthew records Jesus saying, 'My soul is very sorrowful, even to death; remain here, and watch with me' (Matt. 26:38; cf. Mark 14:34).

Jesus was 'sorrowful,' but not merely sorrowful, but by his own words, 'very sorrowful,' using a compound form of the verb (*lupōs*, now *perilupōs*), which indicates, according to Warfield, 'a mental pain, a distress, which hems in on every side, from which there is no escape … which presses in and besets from every side and therefore leaves no place for defence.'[19] He was 'very sorrowful, *even to death*,' his soul being 'so environed and shut up in sorrows in that he had not a cranny left for comfort to come in at,' says Goodwin.[20] Mark says that Jesus was 'greatly distressed' (Mark 14:33; *ekthambeō*), indicating dismay, dread, and horror. He was 'utterly dismayed,' overcome by soul-crushing and life-terminating sorrow.[21]

[18] Thomas Goodwin, 'Of Christ the Mediator,' *The Works of Thomas Goodwin*, Volumes I-X (1861–66; Eureka, CA: Tansky Publications, 1996), V:276.

[19] Warfield, 'Emotional Life of Our Lord,' 131; Goodwin says *perilupōs* 'signifies an encompassing about with sorrows,' and comparing this with Psalm 18:5 and 40:12 indicates, 'His soul was plunged into them over head and ears, so that he had not so much as a breathing hole' ('Of Christ the Mediator,' V:275).

[20] Goodwin, V:275.

[21] Zerwick, I:156; it indicates, says Goodwin, the extremity of horror, as when men's 'hair stands on end, and their flesh trembles' ('Christ the Mediator,' V:275); Zerwick adds that together with *ekthambeō*, it indicates 'he was seized by horror and distress' (I:156).

It is difficult for us when we think that no one understands our suffering. We might come to church and look around and see all the finely dressed and freshly scrubbed people and conclude that they live pain-free lives. No one here understands what I endure, we might assume. No one here relates to me. Truth is, we really don't know each other. There is pain in every pew and behind every door. Still, I may sense, perhaps my pain is beyond that which everyone else has experienced. How I have suffered! Have *I*? He far more. The pressure of his imminent death brought about sweat like drops of blood (Luke 22:44). Luke tells us that 'there appeared to him an angel from heaven, strengthening him' (Luke 22:43, 44), the implication of which may be that without this form of divine intervention, Jesus might have succumbed to death then and there (John 12:27). Yet he must drink the cup assigned to him, even down to its last dregs (John 18:11).

On the cross itself, we hear the cry of dereliction, 'My God, my God, why have you forsaken me?' (Matt. 27:46; cf. Mark 15:34; Psa. 22:8). 'Surely never sorrow was like unto that sorrow which extorted such a complaint,' exclaims Matthew Henry.[22] 'God hid his face from him, and for awhile withdrew his rod and staff in the darksome valley,' he continues.[23]

> He did not say, '*Why am I scourged?* And why *spit* upon? And why *nailed* upon the cross?' Nor did he say to his

[22] Henry, *Exposition*, on Matthew 27:46.
[23] *Ibid.*, 429.

disciples when they turned their back upon him, *Why have ye forsaken me?* But when his Father stood at a distance, he cried out thus.[24]

I recall the preacher of my youth at First Baptist Church of Dominguez, California, Martin Canavan, passionately quoting first the Aramaic and then the English, '*Eli, Eli, lema sabachthani?* My God, my God, why have you forsaken me?' (Matt. 27:46). I found these words to be deeply moving and yet mysterious. Jesus trusted in God ('*My* God ...') even as he experienced the deepest despair ('Why have you forsaken me?').

When preaching at Urbana some years ago, John Stott (1921–2011) contrasted the detached, unruffled, serene figure of the Buddha with the twisted, tortured figure of Christ upon the cross. The former is removed from the pain and suffering of human life and the latter has fully entered into it. He knew it, he felt it, he experienced it; for love he endured it and with compassion he identifies with fellow sufferers.

Joy

Finally, Jesus experienced *joy*. It is true that the Gospels do not record Jesus laughing or even smiling. Yet he came as one whose arrival was itself 'good news of great joy' (Luke

---

[24] *Ibid.* Henry adds this note: 'He fetched from David's psalms (though he could have expressed himself in his own words), to teach us of what use the word of God is to us, to direct us in prayer, and to recommend to us the use of scripture-expressions in prayer, which will *help our infirmities*.'

2:6). He who counsels others against serving God with a 'gloomy' face surely did not wear one himself (Matt. 6:16). By way of contrast with John the Baptist, Jesus says,

> *For John came neither eating nor drinking, and they say,*
> *'He has a demon.' The Son of Man came eating and drink-*
> *ing, and they say, 'Look at him! A glutton and a drunkard,*
> *a friend of tax collectors and sinners!' Yet wisdom is justified*
> *by her deeds* (Matt. 11:18, 19).

Clearly he enjoyed good food and drink and partook of it generously. Jesus speaks of 'my joy' as an abiding or characteristic experience that he imparts to others—'I give to you' (John 15:11; 17:13). His joy was not the superficial or frivolous or temporary joy of this world, but, says Warfield, 'the deep exaltation of a conqueror setting captives free.' It was 'for the joy that was set before him' that he 'endured the cross' (Heb. 12:2). 'If our Lord was "the Man of Sorrows," Warfield continues, 'he was more profoundly still "the Man of Joy."'[25]

Jesus is one who experienced the full range of human experiences and emotions and who reacts as we react, yet without sin. In addition to quietly weeping (John 11:35), loudly crying (Luke 19:41), deeply sighing (Mark 7:34; 8:12), angrily glaring (Mark 3:5), indignantly speaking (Mark 10:14), righteously raging (John 11:33, 38), he was internally agitated (John 11:33), greatly distressed (Luke 12:50), and

[25] Warfield, 'Emotional Life of Our Lord,' 126.

utterly desolate (Matt. 27:46). We find him hungry (Matt. 4:2), thirsty (John 19:20), and weary (John 4:6). 'Nothing is lacking to make the impression strong that we have before us in Jesus a human being much like ourselves,' Warfield concludes.[26] Again, 'Nothing that is human was alien to him, and all that is human manifested itself in him in perfect proportion and balance.'[27] He was like us 'in every respect ... yet without sin' (Heb. 2:17; 4:15). He came in 'the *likeness* of sinful flesh,' yet sinless (Rom. 8:3).

The Scriptures supply an abundance of testimony to Christ's true humanity. We need not look elsewhere for comfort, understanding, sympathy or support in time of need. Because 'he had to be made like his brethren in every respect,' Jesus is 'a merciful and faithful high priest.' 'Because he himself has suffered ... he is able to help' (Heb. 2:18). He is not *unable* but *able* 'to sympathize with our weakness' as one 'who in every respect has been tempted as we are' (Heb. 4:15). Consequently, we need not look to another who might be perceived of as more accessible and compassionate, rather we may 'with confidence draw near to the throne of grace, that we may receive mercy and find grace to help in time of need' (Heb. 4:16).

[26] *Ibid.*, 139.
[27] *Ibid.*, 141.

8

Sowing and Reaping

GALATIANS 6:7, 8

Be not deceived; God is not mocked: for whatsoever a man soweth, that shall he also reap (KJV).

ON June 7, 2017, the parliament of Iran, the world's foremost state-sponsor of terrorism, was ferociously attacked by Islamic terrorists, killing seventeen and wounding dozens more. 'What goes around comes around,' an old saying goes. 'You will reap what you sow' is the biblical principle.

The preacher of my youth, Martin Canavan, pastor of the First Baptist Church of Dominguez in the Long Beach/Carson area of Southern California, thundered the above verses in the King James Version at a time when I needed to hear them. I can't place the time precisely. I was probably a pre-teen or an early teenager. 'God is not mocked,' he shouted in the course of his sermon. That 'word' struck me. It was the first of many self-authenticating encounters with Scripture that would characterize my spiritual pilgrimage. I *knew* that because God is God, it must be true. He will not be mocked. He will not be outwitted. He will not allow evil to remain unaddressed. We don't get away with anything. We mustn't kid ourselves. 'Whatsoever a man soweth, that shall he also reap.' We will reap exactly what we sow. God will see to it. He will ensure it. Sow to the Spirit and reap eternal life, or sow to the flesh and reap corruption and eternal death. The principle has been expressed like this:

> Sow a thought, reap an act;
> Sow an act, reap a habit;
> Sow a habit, reap a character;
> Sow a character, reap a destiny.

I needed to know that truth as a tween and teenager. I was a child of the '60s. From my point of view the world was beginning to come unglued: race riots, student protests, assassinations, the Vietnam War, the 'sexual revolution' with its 'New Morality,' and the widespread experimentation with drugs. I can recall a large group of fellow junior high students staggering towards me, blurry-eyed, obviously high on drugs. This was 8th grade.[1] This was 1967 and the 'Summer of Love' when the hippies converged on the Haight-Ashbury neighbourhood of San Francisco. 'Turn on, tune in, drop out,' Harvard professor Timothy Leary proclaimed. This was 1968, the year of the assassinations of Robert Kennedy and of Martin Luther King, Jr., of multiple race riots, of the Tet

---

[1] The education level of children aged about 12 to 13.

Offensive in Vietnam, of the riots outside the Democratic National Convention in Chicago, of the Soviet-led Warsaw Pact invasion of Czechoslovakia, and so on. This was 1969 and the Woodstock musical festival attended by 400,000 young people. I was observing my friends getting increasingly worldly and giving themselves to fleshly excess. I saw myself as part of a shrinking Christian and moral minority. Hemlines were going up (the 'miniskirt' was the rage), necklines were plunging. Thoughts passed through my mind about whether I was right to follow the path my family and church had laid out before me. Was there a party going on out there amidst all the turmoil? Was I missing out? My preacher's words hit me, or should I say, flooded me with conviction and certainty. God is God. He is not to be trifled with ('messed with' is probably how I expressed it back then).

Stating the principle

> Do not be deceived: God is not mocked, for whatever one sows, that will he also reap (Gal. 6:7).

'Do not be deceived,' the apostle warns us. Why? Because this is an area in which we would tend to be deceived. We easily convince ourselves that our sins are minor, incidental, no big deal. We are sure that there will be no major consequences. We are eager to believe that God doesn't concern himself with our conduct. The Psalms say of the wicked, 'All his thoughts are, "There is no God,"' or more specifically '"God has forgotten, he has hidden his face, he will never see it'" (Psa. 10:4, 11). 'They say, "How can God know? Is there knowledge in the Most High?"' (Psa. 73:11). They are confident that God isn't paying attention. God doesn't care. If there is a God, he doesn't concern himself with trivial matters such as my behaviour. 'Do not be deceived' about the all-seeing, heart-searching God, says the apostle. 'Our actions when done,' says Matthew Poole, 'are not done with.'[2]

The 'big lie' of all the lies of our popular culture is that one can sin with impunity. Rarely are there any consequences for sin. The drunks are all funny drunks. They are the life of the party, beloved by all. They don't seem to get in automobile wrecks and kill people in the movies, like they do in real life. They don't fail at their work and get fired, like in real life. They don't turn their homes into trauma centres. Immorality as popularly portrayed is always *romantic, glamorous, exciting, air-brushed* fun. Teenagers don't get pregnant, like in the real world. No one gets a sexually transmitted disease. Single mothers don't live in abject poverty. Adultery doesn't lead to divorce and heartbroken children. If there is a divorce, it is happy for all. If there is an abortion, there are no regrets. Life is painless. Sin has no consequences. The whole culture screams at our youth, 'Do what you feel like doing.' If you have an itch, scratch it. If you have a desire, fulfil it. 'Just do it,' the ad campaign urges. Yet listen to what God says: 'Don't be deceived!'

'God is not mocked.' He will not be treated with

---

[2] Poole, *Commentary*, III:660.

contempt. Those who think they can escape God's notice err on an epochal scale. He will not long allow us to defy his authority, mock his laws, or blaspheme his name. There will be a reckoning, whether sooner or later. No one will get away with anything.

Rather, 'Whatever one sows, that will he also reap.' Jesus introduces a universal law by way of an agricultural metaphor, the principle of sowing and reaping. Sow corn and corn will be reaped. Don't expect to sow corn and reap wheat. It will not happen. Ever! We reap whatever we sow. Sow sin, and we will reap death and all the pain that leads up to it. Sow the things of the Spirit and we will reap life and all that accompanies it. 'The expression,' says the Scot John Brown (1784–1858), 'intimates that there shall be a strict conformity between a man's present character and conduct, and his future condition.' The connection between now and then, he says, between this world and the future world, 'is not accidental or arbitrary.'[3]

Sowing the flesh

> *For the one who sows to his own flesh will from the flesh reap corruption, but the one who sows to the Spirit will from the Spirit reap eternal life* (Gal. 6:8).

What does it mean for me to 'sow to (my) own flesh'? Sowing is a metaphor of one's life's activity. Because the

---

[3] John Brown, *Galatians*, A Geneva Commentary (1853; repr. Edinburgh: Banner of Truth Trust, 2001), 338.

apostle presents only two options, it represents that which occupies and dominates one's life. 'Flesh' can indicate the physical body or it can denote fallen human nature. Sowing to the flesh, in this context, means to live so as to satisfy the desires of the physical body, some of which may be legitimate, such as marriage, food and sleep, but may be taken to idolatrous extremes, while others are illegitimate, such as drunkenness, gluttony, sloth, adultery, lying, cheating, and coveting (see Gal. 5:16-21, 24). Live life to fulfil these ends and one is serving the flesh, and *there will be dire consequences.* If I live for now, live for the present, live for pleasure, live for worldly honours, live for material things, live for the transitory and perishing, live for self, I will reap 'corruption' or 'destruction' (NIV). Everlasting ruin will be my inheritance. The harvest may come in this world, or it may come in the next. However, it will come.

My college pastor, Mark Neuenschwander, taught me that the flesh is both *pleasurable* and *progressive.* A young man begins to court a young woman. First time he holds her hand, it is electric. Next time, it's not so exciting. Nervously he puts his arm around her. It's thrilling. Next time, it's not so thrilling. It becomes commonplace. The flesh wants more. The flesh is never satisfied. Drug users need more and more to get the same high. Vacations have to get more exotic. Movies have to get more erotic. There was a time when a 'well-turned' ankle was a pretty exciting sight for a man to see, if we can believe the old cowboy movies.

Now little is left to the imagination, all is exposed, nothing is hidden, nothing is sacred. Comedians have to become more vulgar to get the same laugh, a phenomenon we've witnessed over and over again.

Our contemporaries, by and large, tend to live for the present. Even if they are not grossly immoral they are consumed with the temporal. They are sowing to the flesh. They give no thought to eternity. They pay no attention to their souls. They live for the immediate. They surround themselves with all the creature comforts and forms of entertainment that they can afford. They go from meal to ballgame to a weekend away to new car to new clothes. This is what popular culture encourages. The people on TV and in the movies don't go to church. They don't read the Bible. They don't contemplate or discuss the eternal destiny of their souls. They are all, almost without exception, happy atheists. They live like there is no God, and there are no consequences. The message is: Who needs God? One can be happy, fulfilled, satisfied through the things of this world alone. One does not need the *bread of life*. One does not need *living water*. This world alone fulfils us. There is no empty space in the heart. There is no troubling sense of meaninglessness.

Yet what *really* will they reap from a lifetime of sowing this world? In this life, they will experience a deep, profound angst, an unrelieved sense of purposelessness, of alienation, a troubling sense that surely there is something more to life. In the next world they will reap corruption and the opposite of eternal life, destruction. It is vital that we wake up to what is going on all around us. We and our contemporaries are 'amusing ourselves to death,' as Neil Postman insightfully said.[4] Recognize the consequences of such a life. Sowing to the flesh is not harmless; it is not benign; it is not trivial. It is soul-damning.

Sowing to the Spirit

What does it mean to 'sow to the Spirit'? It means that one devotes oneself to the things of the Spirit, to those things that are spiritual, eternal, and divine. One endeavours to 'walk by the Spirit' so that one might not 'gratify the desires of the flesh' (Gal. 5:16). One is 'led by the Spirit' so that one will not succumb to the 'works of the flesh with its passions and desires.' One 'lives by the Spirit' and 'keeps in step with the Spirit' (Gal. 5:24, 25). One cultivates the 'fruit of the Spirit' (Gal. 5:22, 23). One deliberately sets one's mind on the things above and not on the things below (Col. 3:1, 2). There are corrupt behaviours and attitudes to put off (Col. 3:5-9). There are virtuous characteristics and practices to put on (Col. 3:10, 12-17). We are to sow the characteristics of holy love and the disciplines of public worship, family worship, and private devotions, all three of which are saturated with the word of God and prayer.

---

[4] Neil Postman, *Amusing Ourselves to Death: Public Discourse in the Age of Show Business* (1985; New York: Penguin Books, 2005). This book is among a handful of what I consider essential reading for understanding our world today.

The classic case of sowing to the flesh and reaping destruction must be that of King David. He looked out at a bathing Bathsheba and corrupt thoughts led to corrupt acts, including adultery, deception, and murder. He sowed the wind and reaped the whirlwind (Hos. 8:7). Cascading tragedy followed his self-indulgence as his son Amnon raped his sister Tamar. Absalom murdered Amnon, then led a civil war against David, violated his father's household and was himself killed. Sheba then led a second revolt. David sowed violence and reaped devastation (2 Sam. 11–20). Beware!

On the other hand, Joseph sowed integrity, honesty, faithfulness and purity. Given the opportunity to indulge the same lusts that David would later choose to indulge, Joseph refused and later rose to great heights as a ruler in Egypt. He reaped temporal and external rewards (Gen. 39–50).

Remember, this world is merely a preparation for the next. Sow to the spirit, not the flesh. Concentrate on believing and obeying God, on cultivating the fruit of the Spirit and forsaking the deeds of the flesh. Remember that there is no profit in gaining the whole world, with all its prestige, power, pleasure, if we lose our own souls in the process (Matt. 16:26). 'Paul is reminding the Galatians that they should get their priorities right and give time and energy to that which concerns ultimate issues,' says Leon Morris, 'and not merely the passing things of here and now.'[5]

---

[5] Leon Morris, *Galatians: Paul's Charter of Christian Freedom* (Downers

The apostle adds this concluding word of encouragement to his first readers, and to us as well: 'And let us not grow weary of doing good, for in due season we will reap, if we do not give up' (Gal. 6:9).

We are not to 'grow weary' of 'doing good.' We are not to 'give up.' Why might we? Because often the harvest we long for is long delayed, both in terms of abundant life here (John 10:10) and eternal life hereafter. We have so many duties to perform, so many commands to obey, so many pains to endure, and so many temptations to avoid. We grow weary. The reward is slow in coming. Yet we will reap in 'due season.' 'We must not look to sow and reap in a day,' warns John Trapp.[6] In the meantime we must reckon with missing out. The party is inside and we're outside. Fun is to be had and we're not having it. We grow weary. So to meet our discouragement the apostle promises 'we will reap.' Yet we must not 'give up.' The harvest is coming, though it is not yet.

These themes had much to do with keeping me out of trouble at a time when so many of my peers were spiralling out of control. I needed to hear those warnings. I needed to hear about consequences. I believed John 3:16 and 14:6 with all my heart. I believed in salvation by faith in Christ apart from works. Yet I needed a strong dose of biblical realism.

Grove, IL: InterVarsity Press, 1996), 183.

  [6] John Trapp, *A Commentary of the Old and New Testaments*, Vols. I-V. (1647, 1865–68; Eureka, CA: Tansky Publications, 1997), V:587.

Many voices today brush aside this kind of message as 'law' or 'moralism,' thinking to invalidate exhortative preaching as they do. What I'm saying is, I needed to hear Galatians 6:7-9, and I needed to hear it without equivocation, without it being explained away, and without it dying the death of a thousand qualifications. I suppose it is reasonable to believe that God put those verses in his Bible *because we all need to hear them.* I will always be grateful for a preacher who not only preached the gospel, but also preached the Bible's warnings. I needed both, and I suspect we all do as well.

9

Commandments and Obedience

1 JOHN 2:4

Whoever says 'I know him' but does not keep his commandments is a liar, and the truth is not in him.

As a still immature, but growing Christian, I had solidified my understanding of the gospel of free grace in Christ, Romans 4:5 playing a decisive role. Yet I was still troubled by what my Christian friends and I had come to call derisively 'Orange County Christianity': miles wide, inches deep. While others fretted about legalistic fundamentalism (no smoking, drinking, or going to movies), I was disturbed by antinomian fundamentalism, cheap grace and easy-believism.

I had encountered far too many professing believers who were confident of their salvation because of a 'decision' they had made years ago at an evangelistic meeting, who yet were carnal. They showed little regard for Christian disciplines (church attendance, Bible reading, prayer) and little concern for holiness. They were morally sloppy. They showed little integrity. They were indistinguishable from the world and, at times, even compared with worldlings unfavourably. They were less honest, more materialistic, obsessed with cars and houses and wardrobes and physical beauty, as likely to divorce, and pursuing temporal rewards as eagerly as any pagan.

What was I to make of them? Though they claimed to have 'accepted' Christ (their favourite way of expressing their Christian experience), I doubted that their claim could be genuine.

Significant clarification came while attending the Grace Community Church in Panorama City, California. The pastor, John MacArthur, was preaching in the evenings through 1 John. The messages were overwhelming. I had never heard preaching like his: simple, but profound; biblical yet theological; textual yet personal; expository yet applicatory; intellectual yet intense. Every week I walked in one person and walked out another, with new eyes, new outlook, a new perspective on life. At the time he happened to be hammering away at 1 John 2:4. 'Whoever says "I know him" but does not keep his commandments is a liar, and the truth is not in him.' As his exposition unfolded (none of the particulars of which I can remember), the pieces began to fall into place.

The adversaries

The apostle John seems to be quoting the opposition. Who are these 'whoever' who say what he rejects? They are professing Christians. They are or were members of the church. The historians identify them as gnostics or proto-gnostics. They placed a premium on knowledge, particularly mystical or speculative knowledge. At the same time, they deprecated the body and the physical world. The body and its appetites were seen either as a barrier to spiritual progress and consequently to be suppressed, or as irrelevant and therefore safely indulged. Either way, knowledge was thought to be crucial, yet it was knowledge or experience unrelated to moral conduct. Religion, as taught by them, was divorced from ethics. This separation, this gap between the religious and the ethical, was commonplace in the ancient world. Religion was one thing, morals something quite different.

We are seeing a revival of a form of gnosticism today in popular western culture. There is a short step between saying that the physical is secondary, which is true, to saying the physical is irrelevant, that it's only what's inside that counts. The modern gnostic may be heard saying it does not matter what one does with one's body because it's 'only physical' and doesn't touch the 'real' me. Secular forms of gnosticism clearly are evident in the transgender phenomenon and gay marriage. The body is treated as something external to the person, a mere tool of self-expression. Identity is seen as wholly located in the internal self, a 'self' uninformed by the body. The physiology of the body is treated as irrelevant: hence, I may see myself as a woman trapped in the body of a man, or as a man made for erotic relations with other men, again, despite the biology. Even such relatively innocuous phenomena such as scarring, piercing, and tattooing reflect the new outlook. The body is seen not as a sacred and integral part of who I am (the Christian view), but as a mere billboard for self-expression and self-gratification.[1]

The relevance of our passage is obvious. The new gnosticism is infecting the Christian community. Alarming rates of promiscuity can be found even in the so-called conservative churches today. The commands of Christ are being approached cafeteria-style, with self-identifying believers picking and choosing which they will honour. 'It's what's inside that counts.' What matters is loving others. That is what is vital, not what I do with my own body.

Their false claim

The fraudulent claim the apostle John identifies is that 'I know him,' yet I don't 'keep the commandments.' I know God. I know Christ. I have personal, experiential knowledge of Christ. I have a *relationship* with Christ. Yet I don't bother to obey God's commands. Oh, I keep some of them. But I'm indifferent about others. Obedience to commands is not a priority. It is not characteristic of my life. I don't 'keep'

---

[1] See Robert P. George, 'Gnostic Liberalism' in *First Things,* December 2016. See also the many publications of Peter Jones.

them, the Greek present tense indicating habitual conduct. Rather, disobedience is typical and commonplace. I obey what suits my preferences. I ignore the rest. Whereas Jesus says, 'If you love me you will keep my commandments,' I say I love him and disregard the commandments (John 14:15). Whereas Jesus says that whoever keeps and teaches even the least of the commandments shall be called great in the kingdom of heaven, I say that the minor, second-ary commands (as I perceive them to be) can be relaxed or ignored (Matt. 5:19). Whereas Jesus calls for extraordinary measures, the cutting off of the right hand and plucking out of the right eye in order to avoid sin and hell, I find that approach to be excessively serious and legalistic (Matt. 5:29, 30).

The apostle's verdict

The apostle's verdict? Such a one 'is a liar.' John is that blunt and categorical. He leaves zero wiggle room. Miss the point? He adds: 'and the truth is not in him.' The commandment-breaker's claim to know God is false. It's fraudulent. It cannot be true. It is not credible. He is, says Matthew Poole, 'a false, hypocritical pretender.'[2]

We might wonder at this point how the apostle can make such a judgment. How can he be so emphatic, so sure? Granted, he's an apostle. Still, how can he know what is going on inside people's hearts?

[2] Poole, *Commentary*, III:931.

Behind the apostle's certainty is an infallible connection between the *knowledge* of God and *obedience* to God. He is arguing from *effects* (obedience or lack thereof) to *causes* (true knowledge of God or lack thereof). Listen to the previous verse: 'And by this we know that we have come to know him, if we keep his commandments' (1 John 2:3). The apostle John is concerned about both self-doubt and self-deception. He wants to strengthen the faith of the former and undermine the presumption of the latter. 'By this we know,' he says. Here is how we can be certain. Here's how those who might be anxious, or unsure, or confused about the Christian experience can be sure. Am I a real believer? What about these others? The apostle John's response is, do you keep the commandments? Are you a commandment-keeper? Obedience is being cited by the apostle as one of the '*signs* of grace,' as our Puritan forefathers called them. Obedience is a *sign* of the Holy Spirit's presence in a person's life, a *sign* of his gracious work. Do I obey God, not perfectly, not flawlessly, but characteristically, or typically? This is what the older commentators call the 'evangelical keeping of God's commandments,' as John Trapp puts it, in which God measures 'the deed by the desire, and the desire by the sincerity thereof,' when our obedience is rendered through Christ who is our propitiation.[3] Is this the pattern in my life? Obedience should be understood, not as a *condition* to be *fulfilled*, but as a *characteristic* that may be *recognized*.

[3] Trapp, *Commentary*, V:726.

However, for the self-deceived, the failure to keep the commandments, a characteristic and habitual failure, is a sign of the absence of grace. The claim to know Christ by one whose life is devoid of obedience is a false claim, a presumption that the apostle endeavours to undermine.

A further assumption behind the foregoing connection is the transforming power of the gospel. When Christ is received by faith, dynamic change results. The benefits of redemption do not begin upon our arrival in heaven. They are immediate. We are united by faith to Christ in his death to sin and sin's power, and raised up 'in newness of life' (Rom. 6:3). Sin no longer has 'dominion' or control over believers (Rom. 6:14). It 'shall not be master over you' (NASB). We become a 'new creation' in Christ: 'the old has passed away … the new has come' (2 Cor. 5:17). This transformation results in a love of God, of holiness, of righteousness, and of God's command-ments. New affections take hold. New desires, new loves take root. The Holy Spirit comes to dwell within, whose power is perfected in our weakness (2 Cor. 12:9). This love of God and the things of God is 'shed abroad' (KJV) or 'poured into our hearts through the Holy Spirit' (Rom. 5:5), resulting in obedience, as the apostle John concludes: 'but whoever keeps his word, in him truly the love of God is perfected. By this we may know that we are in him' (1 John 2:5).

It is in those who 'keep' God's *word*, a more comprehen-sive term than 'commandment,' signifying all that God has revealed, that 'the love of God,' meaning love *for* God, is 'perfected,' or completed. If I love God, I will want to please him and honour him and serve him. I will want to keep his word and obey him. Jesus said simply, 'If you love me, you will keep my commandments' (John 14:15; 14:21, 23).

Obedience is not the only sign of this perfected love and knowledge. The apostle John also points to a host of other signs: walking in the light (1 John 1:7); confession of sin (1 John 1:8, 9); love for the brethren (1 John 2:7-11; 3:10, 11, 14-18; 4:7–5:2); the affirmation that Jesus is the Christ (1 John 4:2, 3; 5:1-3, 5-12). Yet all these together are in one sense simply obedience (1 John 5:1-3), what the apostle Paul calls 'the obedience of faith' (Rom. 1:5; 16:26; cf. 1 Pet. 1:22; 4:17; Heb. 5:9). 'Godliness and holiness of life distinguish true faith from a fictitious and dead knowledge of God,' says Calvin.[4] This is always the case because the gospel imparts both the *desire* and *capacity* to keep the commandments of God. The apostle John relentlessly pursues this theme of obedience to commandments. 'We know,' he says. 'By this we know that we love the children of God, when we love God and obey his commandments' (1 John 5:2). We have confidence, assurance, certainty about our love for God's children which, remember, he has already presented as a 'sign of grace' (e.g. 1 John 2:7-11; 3:10, 11, 14-18; 4:7, 8, etc.). How? When do we have this confidence? On what basis?

---

[4] John Calvin, *The Gospel According to St John*, Volumes I & II, Calvin's Commentaries translated by T. H. L. Parker; edited by David W. and Thomas F. Torrance (Grand Rapids: William B. Eerdmans Publishing, 1959), II:246.

'When we love God and obey his commandments.' Love of the brethren and obedience to commandments provide a basis for confidence that we truly do love God. Finally, this same apostle identifies the true believers, the 'saints' amidst the tribulations described in his Revelation, as those '… who keep the commandments of God and hold to the testimony of Jesus' (Rev. 12:17; cf. 14:13)

The apostle John's first epistle clarifies the issues for us. The relation between salvation and obedience is now clearer. Salvation inspires and enables, even empowers obedience. Furthermore, the connection between conversion and obedience not only provide grounds for strengthening assurance but also guard us from presumption. This connection also raises concerns for those who profess Christ and yet who defy God's commands.

Orange County Christianity? It is of doubtful authenticity. It appears not to be the real thing. The apostle John warns that it is a counterfeit, made up of people who are either self-deceived or pretending. It is the glory of the gospel that it is life-changing: it changes us. Where there is no change, there is no true Christianity. Thanks be to God that he has not left us in bondage to the flesh, the world and the devil, but has rescued us with a mighty deliverance, resulting in obedience and faithful service.

10

Faith and Works:
Living and Dead Faith

JAMES 2:17

So also faith by itself, if it does not have works, is dead.

THE spiritual environment I lived in as a college student was one in which a person could receive Christ as Saviour and yet not as *Lord*; one in which a third class of persons was created, persons who were neither proper Christians, nor non-Christians, but *carnal* Christians, and, as such, were saved and on their way to heaven, though perpetually worldly;[1] one in which *repentance* was not thought to be necessary for salvation; and one in which the law of God had nothing to say to the believer (denying its 'third' use). These

---

[1] Campus Crusade for Christ literature featured the 'carnal Christian' prominently. What we used to refer to as the 'bird book'—a booklet on the Holy Spirit—featured two diagrams of the human heart in which there was a throne. Christ was on the throne of the Spirit-filled believer, self was on the throne of the carnal Christian.

views were thought to be necessary to guard the grace of the gospel from any intrusions of 'works' or legalism. If we are saved by faith alone, it was said, it cannot be that commitment to the Lordship of Christ, or repentance, or obedience could in any way be required. To demand anything more than bare faith, further reduced to intellectual assent, was thought to introduce works and destroy the gospel.

This view came into open conflict when John MacArthur published his *The Gospel According to Jesus* in 1988. A debate erupted known as the 'Lordship Controversy' and resulted in considerable blow-back; for example, MacArthur was dropped by the Bible Broadcasting Network.[2] The roots of the controversy go back at least to the founder of Dallas Theological Seminary, Lewis Sperry Chafer (1871–1952), and his books, *He That Is Spiritual* (1918) and *Systematic Theology* (1948). His view was perpetuated in more recent times by Dallas Theological Seminary professors Charles C. Ryrie (1925–2016), *Balancing the Christian Life* (1969), his widely utilized *Ryrie Study Bible* (1976), and Zane Hodges, *The Gospel Under Siege* (1981). This 'Saviour but not Lord' scheme, James Montgomery Boice (1938–2000) maintained, 'reduces the gospel to the mere fact of Christ's having died for sinners' and 'requires of sinners only that they acknowledge this by the barest intellectual assent.'[3]

---

[2] John MacArthur, *The Gospel According to Jesus* (Grand Rapids: Zondervan Publishing House, 1988). Both J. I. Packer and J. M. Boice provided forewords.

[3] *Ibid.*, xi.

During my senior year of college (1977), I found myself in a heated argument with a Fuller Seminary student about whether or not obedience could serve as a test of the authenticity of faith, as I had become convinced it must be from 1 John 2:4. It was my first encounter with what I would one day call a 'grace boy.' He would not allow any tests of faith at all. Neither could he countenance repentance as part of the saving response to Christ, nor the necessity of recognizing the Lordship of Christ. He refused to recognize any New Testament concern for those who might be self-deceived, who might be the rocky or shallow soil in whom what appears as healthy growth proves to be superficial and temporary, who fall away under the pressure of 'tribulation or persecution,' though initially they receive the word 'with joy' (Matt. 13:20, 21); or who might be thorny soil, soil overrun with weeds, who also initially receive the word but for whom 'the cares of the world and the deceitfulness of riches choke the word, and it proves unfruitful' (Matt. 13:22).

In the course of the argument, I invoked James: 'faith without works is dead' (James 2:17). All he could hear was the compromise of the gospel. Each time I insisted on good works flowing from true faith, he heard salvation by works. Round and round we went. He went away angry and I frustrated, but determined. A few days later I drove my undergraduate self over to the Fuller Seminary library in Pasadena, California and pulled off the shelves multiple commentaries on James. I took notes, went home, typed up a multi-page response proving my position (or so I thought) and mailed it to my foe.

James, the brother of Jesus, was a 'pillar' of the Jerusalem church, says the apostle Paul, and in this debate he was my friend (Acts 15:13ff.; Gal. 2:9). His second chapter put the final nail in the coffin of my confusion about faith and works. Though James 2:14ff. was at first troubling, ultimately it led to a more coherent and full-orbed understanding of faith.

The tension

James encountered the same sort of problem with which I was wrestling. At first blush, he compounds our confusion by seeming to contradict the apostle Paul. Remember, the apostle Paul said:

> For if Abraham was justified by works, he has something to boast about, but not before God. For what does the Scripture say? 'Abraham believed God, and it was counted to him as righteousness' (Rom. 4:2, 3).

Yet, James says of the same Abraham, 'Was not Abraham our father justified by works when he offered up his son Isaac on the altar?' (James 2:21). The lesson he draws from the life of Abraham is this: 'You see that a person is justified by works and not by faith alone' (James 2:24). He also enlists Rahab in his case: 'And in the same way was not also Rahab the prostitute justified by works when she received the messengers and sent them out by another way?' (James

2:25). Leading to his conclusion: 'For as the body apart from the spirit is dead, so also faith apart from works is dead' (James 2:26).

What is one to make of this? Does the Bible contradict itself? Do Paul and James teach different gospels? Paul says Abraham was *not* justified by works. James says he *was*. One can understand (but not endorse) why a frustrated Luther would refer to James' letter as 'an epistle of straw.'

Differing definitions

Yet the contrast between the apostle Paul and James is not so great as first appears. The key is found in verse 14: 'What good is it, my brothers, if someone says he has faith but does not have works? Can that faith save him?'

The issue addressed by James is what 'someone *says*.' A claim is being made. What claim? The claim to have faith and yet lack accompanying good works. The question being raised is, 'Can *that* faith save him?' What faith? A faith that is fruitless, a faith that 'does not have works,' a faith that does not produce change, a faith that is no more than intellectual assent to doctrines. The key, then, is that James is utilizing a different working definition of faith than the apostle Paul. Whose definition? The watered-down version of his opponents, the 'someone who says.' 'In this whole discourse,' says the Puritan Thomas Manton (1620–77) in his classic exposition of James, 'the apostle's intent is to show, not *what justifieth*, but *who is justified*; not what faith *doth*, but what faith *is*.'[4] What, then, are the qualities of true, that is, justifying faith? James provides three tests.

Demonstrated by good works

First, Jesus insists that true faith may be demonstrated by works. Good works such as love, charity, and morality are the 'fruits and evidences' of true faith, says the *Westminster Confession of Faith* (XVI.2). 'The drift of the context,' says Manton, 'is not to show that faith without works doth not justify, but that a persuasion or assent without works *is not faith*.'[5] James presents a case study on words-only generosity:

> If a brother or sister is poorly clothed and lacking in daily food, and one of you says to them, 'Go in peace, be warmed and filled,' without giving them the things needed for the body, what good is that? So also faith by itself, if it does not have works, is dead (James 2:15-17).

James provides an example to demonstrate the futility of a 'faith' that lacks works. A destitute fellow believer lacks clothing and food. Your response is words: 'Go, be warmed and filled.' Will your words put clothes on his back and food in his belly? Have your words done any good? Of course not. Just as we don't count what Manton calls 'cheap words and charitable wishes' as generosity, God doesn't count mere

---

[4] Thomas Manton, *A Commentary on James*, A Geneva Series Commentary (1693; repr. Edinburgh: Banner of Truth Trust, 1988), comments on James 2:18, 232.

[5] *Ibid.*, 232.

words or bare assent as faith. The point: 'A naked profession of faith is no better than verbal charity.'[6] A faith that lacks good works is 'dead,' James insists. Manton cites the Protestant principle, *sola fides justificat, sed non fides quae est sola*: faith alone justifies, but not faith that is alone. We find the same principle in the apostle John's first epistle:

> *But if anyone has the world's goods and sees his brother in need, yet closes his heart against him, how does God's love abide in him? Little children, let us not love in word or talk but in deed and in truth* (1 John 3:17, 18).

True love, like true faith, will produce good works. 'True faith,' says the Puritan William Gurnall (1616–79) in his classic *The Christian in Complete Armour*, citing James 2, 'is of a working, stirring nature.'[7] Love that merely consists of 'word or talk' is not love 'in truth.' It is counterfeit love. True religion, 'religion that is pure and undefiled before God the Father is this: to visit orphans and widows in their affliction, and to keep oneself unstained from the world' (James 1:27). Good works, says Manton, 'are a proper, perpetual, and inseparable effect of faith.'[8]

> *But someone will say, 'You have faith and I have works.' Show me your faith apart from your works, and I will show you my faith by my works* (James 2:18).

[6] *Ibid.*, 235, 237.
[7] William Gurnall, *The Christian in Complete Armour* (1662 and 1665; repr. London: Banner of Truth Trust, 1964). I:59.
[8] Manton, *James*, 243.

James envisions a third party seeking clarification, claiming, 'You have faith and I have works.' That is, can we say that we each have our strengths and that there is no sense getting in a fuss about it? You have a gift for unshakable *trust*, I for *works* of mercy.[9] No, the problem is that all true believers have saving faith and all true believers have good works which are the fruit of their saving faith. 'Show me your faith apart from works' is 'a kind of ironical expression,' says Matthew Poole.[10] His point is clear enough. 'I will show you my faith *by my works*.' Causes are known by their effects. Works are the fruit, the sign, the evidence, the testimony of saving faith, yet are not themselves meritorious. Faith can be, and must be, demonstrated to be present, active, alive and genuine by the fruit of good deeds.

James does not stand alone in insisting that good works must flow from true faith. The apostle Paul concurs, insisting that 'faith' works 'through love' (Gal. 5:6). Faith *works*. Those who are saved by Christ, saved by grace through faith 'are God's workmanship, created in Christ Jesus *for good works*' (Eph. 2:10). Believers are devoted to *good works* (Titus 3:8). The apostle Paul connects grace, atonement, and good works in Titus 2:11-14.

> *For the grace of God has appeared, bringing salvation for*
> *all people, training us to renounce ungodliness and worldly*

---

[9] See Alec Motyer, *The Message of James: The Tests of Faith* (Downers Grove, IL: InterVarsity Press, 1985), 112.
[10] Poole, *Commentary*, III:887.

*passions, and to live self-controlled, upright, and godly lives
in the present age, waiting for our blessed hope, the appear-
ing of the glory of our great God and Saviour Jesus Christ,
who gave himself for us to redeem us from all lawlessness and
to purify for himself a people for his own possession who are
zealous for good works.*

'Grace,' he says, trains us 'to renounce ungodliness' and
so on. Christ 'gave himself to redeem us' from what? From
'lawlessness' and to 'purify' us and create a people who are
'zealous for *good works.*' James and Paul agree. True faith
produces the fruit of good works. Jesus says, 'I chose you
and appointed you'—to what end? He continues, 'that you
should go and *bear fruit* and that your fruit should abide'
(John 15:16). Jesus teaches, 'You will recognize them *by their
fruits*' (Matt. 7:20).

*Beware of false prophets, who come to you in sheep's clothing
but inwardly are ravenous wolves. You will recognize them
by their fruits. Are grapes gathered from thorn bushes, or
figs from thistles? So, every healthy tree bears good fruit, but
the diseased tree bears bad fruit. A healthy tree cannot bear
bad fruit, nor can a diseased tree bear good fruit. Every tree
that does not bear good fruit is cut down and thrown into
the fire. Thus you will recognize them by their fruits* (Matt.
7:15-20).

We don't expect to pick apples from lemon trees. We
know by the fruit the nature of the tree: if apples, an apple
tree; if oranges, an orange tree; if healthy fruit, a healthy

tree; if unhealthy fruit, an unhealthy tree. Behavioural 'fruit' reveals the person's nature. Actions betray whether a sheep is a sheep or a wolf dressed as a sheep. The assumption in James is the same as we saw in the previous chapter in 1 John. A believing encounter with Jesus Christ is life-transforming. The fruit of good works inevitably grows.[11]

Finally, it is *because* works are the *fruit* of faith that they can serve as a *test* of faith. The ascended Christ repeatedly assesses the seven churches on the basis of their works. 'I know your *works*,' he says repeatedly (Rev. 2:2, 19; 3:1, 8, 15). The ascended Lord Christ commends the good works of patient endurance and perseverance (Rev. 2:2, 3); of love, faith, and service (Rev. 2:19), and of faithfulness (Rev. 3:9). He also exhorts those who are slipping to 'do the *works* you did at first' (Rev. 2:5); and urges those whom he has 'not found (their) *works* complete' to 'wake up' and repent (Rev. 3:3), or to 'be zealous and repent' (Rev. 3:19). The ascended

---

[11] Using similar language, John Owen affirms 'the necessity of good works, notwithstanding that we are not saved by them' ('Of Communion with God,' *The Works of John Owen*, Volumes 1-16 [1674, 1850–53; repr. London: Banner of Truth Trust, 1965], II:182). Indeed, the 'whole work (of the Holy Spirit) upon us, in us, for us, consists in preparing of us for obedience; enabling of us thereunto, and bringing forth the fruits of it in us' (183). While these fruits are only possible in Christ by the power of the Holy Spirit, he speaks not merely of the necessity, but 'the indispensable necessity of our obedience, good works, and personal righteousness,' not as 'the *cause*, *matter*, nor *condition* of our justification,' yet as 'the way appointed of God for us to work for the *obtaining* of salvation' (186-87, emphasis added). Again, 'We are neither justified nor saved without (good works), though we are not justified by them, nor saved for them' ('A Vindication of "On Communion with God,"' *Works*, II:321).

Christ warns that the gifts and rewards of grace are distributed according to works, evaluated internally and externally. 'I am he who searches mind and heart, and I will give to each of you according to your works' (Rev. 2:23; cf. Matt. 16:27; John 5:29; Rom. 2:6; 2 Cor. 5:10; 1 Pet. 1:17).

So certain is the connection between the people of God and good works that the 'bride' of Christ at 'the marriage supper of the Lamb' is dressed in 'fine linen, bright and pure.' Then comes this explanatory line: 'the fine linen is the *righteous deeds of the saints*' (Rev. 19:7-9). Of course these 'righteous deeds' are Christ-enabled and Holy-Spirit-empowered, yet they are the righteous deeds *of the saints*. The 'great white throne' judgment has all humanity, 'great and small,' standing before the throne to be judged 'according to what they had done,' we are told twice (Rev. 20:11-13). 'Done' is the word 'works' (Greek, *erga*), as in the KJV, or 'deeds' in the NASB. Judgment according to *works* or *deeds* indicates not that salvation is according to works or deeds but that our works and deeds will verify or falsify our claims to have justifying faith. Works are the test of faith because good works are the fruit of genuine faith, inevitably and invariably. Is a given claim of saving faith credible? Good works will prove or disprove it. Judgment will not be, 'Have you done enough good works to get in?' The assessment of good works will have nothing to do with merit. Rather, the question will be, Is the faith fruitless assent or transforming trust? This brings us to our next point.

More than mere assent

Second, James goes on and presents a second case study, this one of mere assent to propositions. He identifies one who believes 'that God is one.' Is that enough to save?

> *You believe that God is one; you do well. Even the demons believe—and shudder!* (James 2:19).

His answer is a devastating rebuttal of 'faith' as mere mental assent to doctrine. Believing that 'God is one' is a foundational biblical truth. The Hebrews called it the *shama* (from the Hebrew verb *to hear*): 'Hear O Israel: The LORD our God, the LORD is one' (Deut. 6:4). This is a fundamental article of monotheistic faith. 'You do well' to believe it, says James, again using irony. 'The demons believe,' he says, 'and shudder.'

Yet believing a doctrine as simple as this saves no one. The demons believe the *shama*. They were among the first to acknowledge Jesus' true identity (e.g. Matt. 8:29). Yet faith, by that definition, won't save them. Their belief is not saving belief. It is but intellectual affirmation. 'There is not only *assent* in faith,' says Manton of saving faith, 'but *consent*; not only an assent to the truth of the word, but a consent to take Christ.'[12]

> *Do you want to be shown, you foolish person, that faith apart from works is useless?* (James 2:20).

---

[12] Manton, *James*, 240.

A faith that merely affirms doctrine and doesn't result in good works is 'useless.' It is no more than assent to the obvious. It is not genuine or saving faith. What's missing? Trust. Commitment. Surrender. Repentance. The person who attends church each week, who walks in, takes a seat, affirms the Creed, repeats the Lord's Prayer, listens to the sermon, and walks out at the end of the service and remains unaffected does not have true faith. Nominal assent is not faith.

Put it this way. If I *believe* that the bridge directly ahead of me is going to collapse, will my behaviour be affected? If I truly believe it cannot sustain my weight, my 'faith,' my belief will be demonstrated by my decision not to attempt to cross it. If I have faith that a chair can bear my weight, I will not hesitate to plop down onto it. What we believe always determines what we do and how we act. Belief that Jesus is the pearl of 'great price' will lead to the selling everything in order to buy that most precious of pearls (Matt. 13:45, 46). If I believe that Jesus Christ is the Saviour of the world and Lord of heaven and earth, the consequence will be a faith that consists of total abandonment to Christ, a consent to have him as my Lord; and not merely a bare assent to the doctrine of the gospel that leaves behaviour unaffected.

Historical examples

James supports his case by pointing to two examples of actively working faith from redemptive history: Abraham and Rahab, who represent two extremes of the redemptive spectrum; Abraham, the father of the faithful, Rahab, a pagan prostitute.

> *Was not Abraham our father justified by works when he offered up his son Isaac on the altar? You see that faith was active along with his works, and faith was completed by his works; and the Scripture was fulfilled that says, 'Abraham believed God, and it was counted to him as righteousness'— and he was called a friend of God* (verses 2:21-23).

Verse 23 cites Genesis 15:6, quoted by the apostle Paul in Romans 4 (as we have seen), proving that Abraham was justified by faith. So in what sense was the offering of Isaac an example of justification by works, as claimed by James in verse 21? This is a difficult question, yet it is simplified by remembering that Isaac was offered decades *after* Abraham was 'counted' righteous. Abraham's justification occurs in Genesis 15:6. Isaac was offered thirty years later as recorded in Genesis 22. What, then, was the justification of Genesis 22? It was the justification not of the *person*, but of the *faith*.[13] 'His *faith* itself (was) justified,' says Poole, 'as his *person* was before.'[14] Abraham's claim of faith was justified in the sense of being legitimized, or even verified. The reality of Abraham's faith was proven by offering Isaac as a sacrifice, confirming that it was true and justifying faith.

---

[13] So Manton: 'The justification he speaketh of is not so much of the person as of the faith' (*James*, 232).

[14] Poole, *Commentary*, III:887 (emphasis added).

We might paraphrase verse 21, 'Was not Abraham our father *shown by his works to be a man justified by faith?*' His faith was 'completed' by works, meaning 'made … more fully known and apparent,' says Manton, or even 'bettered and improved.'[15] His faith was an 'active' faith, a living and transforming faith, his works completing his faith in the sense of faith coming to full expression through action. His faith, says Poole, was by works 'approved as a true, lively, justifying faith.'[16] Indeed, 'The design of the apostle is not to show how sinners are justified in God's court, but only what kind of faith it is whereby they are justified.'[17]

The pieces of the puzzle were fitting together for me. Those troubling carnal, worldly Christians and their hyper-grace defenders with whom I was contending, probably were like those James combatted. We are saved by faith alone. Yet what is faith? It is not mere assent to doctrines. Their claim of faith was spurious. How can we know? Because faith without works is dead!

> *You see that a person is justified by works and not by faith alone* (James 2:24).

'Not by faith alone,' we repeat, means 'not by faith that is alone.' While faith is 'the alone instrument of justification,' the *Westminster Confession of Faith* assures us, 'yet it is not alone in the person justified.' Rather, true faith 'is

---

[15] Manton, *James*, 253, 254.
[16] Poole, *Commentary*, III:887.
[17] *Ibid.*

ever accompanied with all other saving graces' (XI.2). We are not justified by a faith that has no fruit, no works, and that brings about no change, because that 'faith' is not faith.

> *And in the same way was not also Rahab the prostitute justified by works when she received the messengers and sent them out by another way?* (James 2:25).

Rahab, James' second historical example, standing at the other end of the spiritual spectrum from holy Abraham, confessed to the Hebrew spies, 'As soon as we heard it,' that is, of the exodus and the early conquests in Canaan, 'our hearts melted, and there was no spirit left in any man because of you, for the LORD your God, *he is God in the heavens above and on the earth beneath*' (Josh. 2:11). On the basis of this profession of faith in the God of Israel, she hid the spies. 'By faith Rahab …' (Heb. 11:31). Her doing so demonstrated that her words were more than mere words, empty rhetoric. Her faith was not spurious, but real and risky.

And so the conclusion:

> *For as the body apart from the spirit is dead, so also faith apart from works is dead* (James 2:26).

Whether one is Father Abraham or a mere harlot, justifying faith, living faith, saving faith will result in good works. Faith in the absence of good works is 'dead.' 'A carnal Christian,' Manton insists, 'is the carcass of a true Christian.'[18]

[18] Manton, *James*, 270.

Importance

The apostles' concerns, and our concerns, are pastoral: that souls not be put at risk by mistaking true faith for its counterfeit. James urges us to be 'doers of the word and not hearers only,' adding this warning, '*deceiving* yourselves' (James 1:22). This is the pastoral issue. Concern is for those with unwarranted assurance or what Manton calls 'careless security.' He warns: 'To a loose, carnal spirit, an absolute promise is as poison.'[19] Self-deception is a problem among professing Christians which must be guarded against. A true believer is 'a doer who *acts*' (James 1:25). He honours what James calls the 'perfect law, the law of liberty' and 'the royal law' (James 1:25; 2:12; 2:8). He isn't picking and choosing among commandments because he knows that

> *whoever keeps the whole law and yet stumbles in one point, he has become guilty of all* (James 2:10, NASB).

Rather, he is 'a doer of the law' (James 4:11). 'Blessed are those who hear the word of God *and keep it*,' Jesus insists (Luke 11:28). Doing is contrasted with mere hearing, genuine faith with mere assent, and both aim to awaken the self-deceived, one Manton calls 'the secure carnalist.'[20]

Remember, the apostle Paul primarily was dealing with Judaizing Christians and self-righteous professing believers, 'whereas,' says Poole, 'James (was) having to do with carnal professors, and such as abused the doctrine of grace

[19] *Ibid.,* 250.
[20] *Ibid.,* 253.

to encourage themselves in sin.'[21] 'Paul pleadeth for saving faith,' says Manton; 'James pleadeth against naked assent.'[22] Consequently, their respective emphases are different. Yet even Paul can warn those who would 'use [their] freedom as an opportunity for the flesh' (Gal. 5:13). After listing a number of the 'works of the flesh' such as sexual immorality, idolatry and drunkenness, he warns, 'Just as I also told you in time past, that those who practise such things will not inherit the kingdom of God' (Gal. 5:21b). Similarly, Jude warns of 'ungodly men, who turn the grace of our God into lewdness and deny the only Lord God and our Lord Jesus Christ.' He classifies them as 'designated for condemnation' (Jude 4). The apostle Peter likewise urges us to 'live as people who are free,' yet 'not using your freedom as a cover-up for evil' (1 Pet. 2:16). There have always been those who would turn grace into cheap grace, and consider the gospel a license to sin with impunity (see Rom. 3:8; 6:1, 2).

Can one receive a divided Christ, one who is Saviour and not Lord? Of course not! Can one receive salvation from him and still stubbornly cling to one's idols and lusts, refusing to relinquish them? Of course not! Can one be a true Christian and yet remain worldly, carnal, defiant, living a life characterized by disobedience and rebellion? Certainly not! The true believer receives the whole Christ. The true

---

[21] Poole, III:888; 'Justification in Paul is opposite to the condemnation of a hypocrite in particular' (Manton, *James*, 246).

[22] Manton, *James*, 264.

believer receives Christ as prophet, priest, and king: a prophet to instruct, a priest to atone, a king to rule. He doesn't divide the offices of Christ. As the Puritan Joseph Alleine (1634–68) argues in *A Sure Guide to Heaven*, 'He seeks not only the *benefits*, but the *burden* of Christ … the *dominion* of Christ as well as the *deliverance*.' However, the counterfeit believer 'takes Christ by halves,' says Alleine. 'He is all for *salvation,* but not *sanctification*. He is all for the *privileges*, but neglects the *person* of Christ.' False believers 'desire salvation from *suffering*, but do not desire to be saved from *sinning* … they are content to destroy some sins, but cannot leave the lap of Delilah.'[23]

Jesus asked, 'Why do you call me "Lord, Lord," and not do what I tell you?' (Luke 6:46). That kind of faith is not living but dead. That kind of knowledge is a lie (1 John 2:4). The gospel is not just words *believed*, bur power *received* (Rom. 1:16). 'The kingdom of God does not consist in talk, but in *power*,' says the apostle Paul (1 Cor. 4:20): transforming power, Holy Spirit power, new creation power, newness of life power.

James and the apostle John help us to clarify what the apostle Paul himself teaches. True faith results in surrender to the Lordship of Christ. True faith lays hold of Christ at the same time as in repentance it turns away from sin. True faith makes permanent carnality impossible. True faith

---

[23] Joseph Alleine, *A Sure Guide to Heaven* (1671; repr. London: Banner of Truth Trust, 1964), 44-46.

results in obedience to commands. True faith bears the fruit of good works. Believers may be found all along the spectrum from carnal to holy. However, no believers may rest passively and contentedly in carnality, and all true believers strive to grow in that holiness without which no one will see the Lord (Heb. 12:14). If this is not my faith, it is best that I know it now while there is time to get right with God.

Here is the bottom line: we are not saved *by* works but *for* them; we are not saved by obedience, but if we love Christ we will keep his commandments (John 15:10). We are not saved by law, but we are meant to fulfil its righteous requirements (Rom. 8:4). Faith, if genuine, *works*. Insisting that works follow faith guards the church from false claims of faith and guards the saints from the self-deception about which Jesus and the apostles were so concerned (Matt. 7:21ff.; 13:1-23; Gal 5:13ff.; 1 John, the whole letter; etc.).

* * *

Works are not a ground of confidence, but an evidence; not the foundations of faith, but the encouragements of assurance. Comfort may be increased by the sight of good works, but it is not built upon them; they are seeds of hope, not props of confidence; sweet evidences of election, not causes; happy presages and beginnings of glory; in short, they can manifest an interest, but not merit it. We have 'peace with God' by the righteousness of Christ, and 'peace of conscience,' by the fruits of righteousness in ourselves (Manton, *James*, on 2:18, 239).

11

The Struggle

ROMANS 7:18-24

For I know that nothing good dwells in me, that is, in my flesh. For I have the desire to do what is right, but not the ability to carry it out. For I do not do the good I want, but the evil I do not want is what I keep on doing … Wretched man that I am! Who will deliver me from this body of death?

'A CERTAIN type of ministry of the gospel is *cruel*,' says Jim Packer (1926–2020), in the opening sentence of 'These Inward Trials,' the twenty-first chapter of *Knowing God*. It doesn't mean to be, he admits, but it is. What kind of ministry is that? It is an evangelical, that is, a Bible-honouring ministry of the kind which I happened to encounter as a junior in college. Yet Packer describes it as so playing down the 'rougher side' of the Christian life 'as to give the impression that normal Christian living is a bed of roses, a state of affairs in which … problems no longer exist.' Or, if problems do come, it insists that one need only trust and pray and 'they will melt away at once.'[1]

Might there be a danger that our own studies have created the impression that the Christian's life of obedience, of keeping the commandments (1 John 2:4) and of doing good works (James 2:14ff.) is something that comes easily to us? When we say that there is a necessary and invariable connection between a true knowledge of God and commandment-keeping, between faith and works, might we be heard as saying that obedience and good works follow without a struggle? Worse, might the struggling Christian conclude that his lack of growth indicates he is not a Christian at all? If so, *our* ministry has become *cruel*.

Personal experience

The struggling Christian, Packer continues, wrongly taught to 'regard all experiences of frustration and perplexity as signs of sub-standard Christianity,' now encounters 'further bondage by the strait-jacket of a remedy by which it proposes to dispel these experiences.' Struggle, according to this 'cruel' type of ministry, is equalled with defeat, caused by a failure of 'consecration' or 'trust,' the cure of which is found in confession and reconsecration. 'If he does this (it is affirmed), he will find himself once more, in the theological as well as metaphorical sense, on top of the world,' Packer explains.[2]

[1] J. I. Packer, *Knowing God* (Downers Grove, IL: InterVarsity Press, 1973), 221, 222.
[2] *Ibid.*, 224, 225.

My own problem was that the exciting and rapid growth of my sophomore year of college was followed by a dark junior year of struggle. As a now serious Christian, I didn't know where I belonged any longer. I was living in a fraternity house, alienated by a brotherhood whose common bond seemed to be debauchery. I didn't mind the excesses of 'Greek' life the year before. Now I did. The 'brothers' seemed to sense my discomfort and resented it. I felt ostracized, alone, isolated.

I was struggling with my own heart-sins as well. I was discouraged by my lack of progress in the Christian life. I saw great joy and peace in other serious Christians, little in me, and wondered how I could be Christian at all when I was so unsettled much of the time? For most of my adult life I have been a happy person. I don't worry much. I don't get down. I whistle and sing a lot. I am at peace. I'm blessed with joy and contentment. But not then. I was down, and to use a word tossed around far too much, I was *depressed*.

My Christian friends responded mostly by telling me to get over it. They hinted that I was being a bad witness. If the Christian life was as gloomy as I made it seem, who would want to become a believer? I was urged to be filled with the Spirit, and since the fruit of the Spirit is peace and joy, such would return to me. I was given the little blue 'bird book' that I mentioned in the last chapter, in which I was taught 'spiritual breathing.' Breathe out sin through confession, breath in the Spirit by asking, 'Fill me with your Spirit,' as

Ephesians 5:18 requires. It's God's will for us to be 'filled.' We've prayed according to God's will. Consequently, I was told, we have it. Trust that it is done. You are now filled. It is that simple, even mechanical. My mistake, I was assured, was that I was striving. Why all this stress and strain? Why the morbid introspection and self-doubt? I needed to stop. I needed only to yield, to 'let go and let God,' and all would be well again. Just abide. 'Allow' God to work. Just hand it over to him and he'd win the victory for me. If I simply surrendered to Christ, he would fight my battles and all would be struggle-free peace and joy.

The result of this counsel from Job's friends: my despondency compounded. Now I was not only down, but I was ruining my Christian witness and dampening the impact of Christian outreach, the realization of which cast me further and further into darkness. I was caught in a downward spiral, discouraged because I was discouraged, from which I feared I would not recover.

Romans 7

One day my Christian friends and I were reading a Campus Crusade booklet, *Ten Basic Steps Toward Christian Maturity*, specifically Step 3, 'The Christian and the Holy Spirit,' and happened upon a citation from Romans 7. Here are some highlights:

> *For I do not understand my own actions. For I do not do what I want, but I do the very thing I hate.*

For I know that nothing good dwells in me, that is, in my flesh. For I have the desire to do what is right, but not the ability to carry it out. For I do not do the good I want, but the evil I do not want is what I keep on doing.

For I delight in the law of God, in my inner being, but I see in my members another law waging war against the law of my mind and making me captive to the law of sin that dwells in my members. Wretched man that I am! Who will deliver me from this body of death?

(Rom. 7:15, 18, 19, 22-24)

As we read these verses I had a *eureka* moment. That's me, I said to myself. The apostle's struggle deeply resonated with me. I want to do what is right. Yet, 'I do the very thing I hate.' Yes, I do hate my sin. I 'have the *desire* to do what is right, but not the *ability*.' 'I do not do the good I *want*, but the evil *I do not want* is what I keep on doing.' The apostle is describing me. I am this weak, torn, conflicted, foolish person. I am the 'wretched man.' Our study leader explained that Romans 7 was the apostle Paul's pre-Christian testimony and we needed to move on to Romans 8. Yet instinctively I knew better. As the Scottish pastor/theologian Alexander Whyte (1836–1921) said to his congregation, 'You'll never get out of the seventh of Romans while I'm your minister.'[3] Indeed, we never do. We never escape the fight. We never arrive. Yet despite our

---

[3] C. F. Barbour, *The Life of Alexander Whyte* (London: Hodder and Stoughton, 1925), 305.

divided minds and flawed lives, there is 'no condemnation' for those in Christ Jesus (Rom. 8:1).

What are the implications of Romans 7? Let me explain.

Perfectionism

First, Romans 7 rebuts any notion of 'complete sanctification' or perfectionism. B. B. Warfield, the 'Lion of old Princeton' (1851–1921), wrote over a thousand pages on 'Perfectionism' between 1918 and 1921.[4] He devoted the last three years of his life to exposing its harmful flaws. Though there are various forms of perfectionism and semi-perfectionism, they all originate as a reaction against what was called 'miserable sinner Christianity': gloomy, defeated, morbid, sin-obsessed, failure-focused forms of Christianity. Essentially what perfectionists say (or imply) in common is that the Christian life consists of two distinct acts of faith. By the first we are justified as we place our faith in Christ alone for salvation. Yet there is a second act of faith by which we receive the second blessing of full and complete sanctification. This is the 'secret' of the Christian life, they say, which so many others have missed. Those 'others' are genuine Christians, just not Spirit-filled.

Consequently, there are two classes of Christians: carnal and mature. If the carnal Christians would just learn to trust, to yield to God, they would no longer struggle with sin; they would enjoy perfect peace, joy, and contentment.

[4] B. B. Warfield, *Perfectionism,* Volumes 1 & 2 (New York: Oxford University Press, 1931).

As we walk in the Spirit we will no longer carry out the desires of the flesh (as in Rom. 8:4ff. and Gal. 5:16, 17). Our aim as Christians, perfectionists maintain, is to reach this plateau, variously known as the 'higher life' or 'victorious life' or 'abundant life.' They ask, can a believer avoid sin for a moment? How about two? On and on the moments may be strung for a lifetime. A guest lecturer during my student days at Gordon Conwell Theological Seminary announced that he had not sinned in the previous twenty years, sin having been watered-down and redefined as 'conscious sins' or 'known sins.' Compare this outlook with that of the apostle Paul:

> *Not that I have already obtained this or am already perfect, but I press on to make it my own, because Christ Jesus has made me his own. Brothers, I do not consider that I have made it my own. But one thing I do: forgetting what lies behind and straining forward to what lies ahead, I press on toward the goal for the prize of the upward call of God in Christ Jesus* (Phil. 3:12-14).

'Not that I have already obtained this' or 'attained this' (KJV) *'or am already perfect,'* the 'this' being the completed knowledge of Christ that will be ours in the resurrected or eternal state. 'It belongs to the very essence of Christianity that we have *not* "attained,"' says Warfield, and 'that sancti- fication is in progress and there is more to come.'[5] No, the apostle is not yet 'perfect,' though for that perfected state

---

[5] Warfield, *Perfectionism*, I:91 (emphasis added).

he *does* strive. Jesus held out the goal of perfection when he commanded, 'Be *perfect* as your Father in heaven is perfect' (Matt. 5:48). Yet we will never arrive at perfection in this life. 'I do not consider that I have made it,' the apostle says. 'I *press* on,' he says, 'I *press* toward the goal,' he says again. Warfield quotes Luther with approval—Christians are not 'made' but 'in the making.'[6] We will never be free from the remaining dregs of sin. 'Original corruption,' the *Westminster Confession of Faith* teaches, 'doth remain in those that are regenerated' though 'through Christ, pardoned, and mortified' (VI.4, 5). We are free from the *bondage* of sin (Rom. 6:3ff.), but not the *remnants*. The apostle Paul even says, 'The *evil* I do not want is what I keep doing' (Rom. 7:19). We will always in this world be '*straining forward* to what lies ahead.' Until when? Until glory. Only then will we be glorified.

Expectations are crucial in the Christian life. If I am expecting that if I dot the *i*'s and cross the *t*'s of the Christian life, that I will rise above the struggle, I may be crushed with disappointment and despair by my failure to reach that blissful state. If, however, I am taught that real progress can be made in the Christian life, that substantial victory over sin may be enjoyed, yet that I will never, ever complete that victory, that the fight is lifelong, that I am not only *simul justus et peccator* (both just and sinner) but *semper justus et peccator* (always just and sinner), then I will be armed with

---

[6] Warfield, *Perfectionism*, I:131.

reasonable expectations; then I will understand my struggle to be normal and lifelong; then I will not become despondent. Rather, I will always understand that I am still the 'chief of sinners' (1 Tim. 1:15, KJV).

'Sanctification,' the *Confession* teaches, is 'imperfect in this life, there abiding still some remnants of corruption in every part, whence ariseth a continual and irreconcilable war, the flesh lusting against the Spirit, and the Spirit against the flesh' (XIII.2). 'When sin lets us alone,' says John Owen (1616–1683) in his masterpiece, *The Mortification of Sin*, 'we may let sin alone,' and we might add, and not before.[7] As Luther said in the first of his Ninety-five Theses, the whole life of believers, from beginning to end, from top to bottom, is a life of repentance. The wise old *Heidelberg Catechism* asks in connection with the Ten Commandments, 'Can those who are converted to God perfectly keep these commandments?' It answers (in part), 'No, but even the holiest men, while in this life, have only a small beginning of this obedience.'

Passivity

Romans 7 also rebuts passivity, the kissing-cousin of perfectionism. If I can conquer sin completely, then the fight against sin is over. Perfectionism loses sight of the struggle and encourages a kind of passivistic piety. This is sanctification by

---

[7] John Owen, *The Mortification of Sin* (1656, 1678; repr. Edinburgh: Banner of Truth Trust, 2022), 10.

realization. Realization of what? That the victory is already won by Christ. As we are justified by faith, so also are we sanctified by faith. One need only trust God to do the fighting. He battles. God takes care of defeating sin for us. He fights our fight. All we must do is yield to him. Our job, as already noted, is to 'let go and let God.' God does it all.

Yet, Romans 7 is followed by Romans 8, as the perfectionists have pointed out, though not for the reasons which we will cite. The celebration of victory over sin in Romans 8:1-4 yields to the sober reality of Romans 8:5-13. There the apostle Paul calls us by the Spirit to 'put to death the deeds of the body' (Rom. 8:13; cf. Col. 3:5). The old word for this was 'mortify.' The apostle uses active language. His words indicate continuous, vigorous exertions. Moreover, mortification, says Owen, is a daily work. 'Cease not a day from this work,' he warns. 'Be killing sin, or it will be killing you.'[8]

'*Strive* to enter through the narrow door,' Jesus urges, utilizing terminology despised by the perfectionists (Luke 13:24). The word translated 'strive' (*agōnizomai,* to struggle) is used seven times in the New Testament, each in a positive sense. Describing his ministry, the apostle Paul says, 'I toil, *struggling* with all his energy that he powerfully works within me' (Col. 1:29). God supplies the energy, we toil and struggle. We 'toil and *strive,*' he insists (1 Tim. 4:10). He describes prayer as '*struggling* on your behalf' (Col. 4:12). To Timothy he characterizes the whole Christian life as

[8] *Ibid.,* 9.

a fight: '*Fight* the good *fight* of faith,' or literally 'struggle (*agōnizomai*) the good struggle (*agōn*) of faith' (1 Tim. 6:12; 2 Tim. 4:7). Living the Christian life is a fight undertaken by faith, but it is a fight, it is a struggle. It is not easy. We 'struggle against sin' (Heb. 12:4, *antagonizomai*).

Activistic language is used throughout the New Testament as we are urged to '*put off*' sin and '*put on*' righteousness (Rom. 13:12-14; Eph. 4:22-24ff.; Col. 3:8-12). We are to '*flee*' immorality (1 Cor. 6:18) and '*pursue*' righteousness (1 Tim. 6:11; 2 Tim. 2:22); to '*hold fast*' to our 'confession' and 'hope' (Heb. 4:14; 6:18; 10:23; 1 Cor. 15:2; Rev. 3:11); to 'be *diligent*' (*spoudazō*), a term applied five times to the Christian life. We are urged to be *diligent* to enter our eternal rest lest we fall away (Heb. 4:11); and 'be *diligent*' to be found in Christ without spot or blemish (2 Pet. 3:14) and 'be all the more *diligent* to make (our) calling and election sure' (2 Pet. 1:10; cf. Eph. 4:3; 1 Thess. 2:13; 2 Tim. 2:15). 'There is no Quietism here,' says Warfield.[9] We must '*resist*' the devil (James 4:7; 1 Pet. 5:9), '*train*' or '*discipline*' (NASB) ourselves for godliness (1 Tim. 4:7), '*stand firm*' (1 Cor. 16:13), '*cleanse* our hands' and '*purify* our hearts' (James 4:8).

Elsewhere the apostle Paul insists that 'those who belong to Christ Jesus have *crucified* the flesh with its passions and desires' (Gal. 5:24). He says of his own commitment to Christ, 'The world has been *crucified* to me, and I to the world' (Gal. 6:14). This is aggressive, violent, vehement

---

[9] Warfield, *Perfectionism*, II:553.

language. His is not a defensive conflict. He is taking the offensive, because as they say in athletic competition, the best defence is a good offence. It is no accident that among the favourite metaphors of the Christian life employed by the apostles are those of athletic competition and military warfare. The apostle Paul likens himself to a boxer who punches with purpose, to a runner who runs 'so as to win,' and to a wrestler (1 Cor. 9:24-27; Eph. 6:12; 2 Tim. 2:5). Likewise the writer to the Hebrews:

> *Therefore, since we are surrounded by so great a cloud of witnesses, let us also lay aside every weight, and sin which clings so closely, and let us run with endurance the race that is set before us* (Heb. 12:1).

The Christian life is like a 'race' to be won by discarding sin and whatever else might inhibit progress and running with 'endurance.' It is also like a war to be fought. The apostle urges us to 'arm ourselves' (1 Pet. 4:1). We wield weapons for warfare (2 Cor. 6:7; 10:4ff.). Because we are 'strong in the Lord and in the strength of his might,' we 'put on the whole armour of God' and go into battle (Eph. 6:10, 11; Rom. 13:1; 2 Cor 6:7). We 'work out our salvation' because 'it is God who works in us' (Phil. 2:12, 13). That God is at work is not an excuse for passivity but a call to arms. Because God is at work, we are able to work out our salvation, and work it out we must. 'We will not be making progress in holiness,' says Owen, 'without walking over the bellies of our lusts.'[10] Anyone who implies that we can arrive in heaven on 'flowery beds of ease' is teaching tragically misleading and harmful doctrine.[11]

Recalibrates normality

Discovering this was liberating for me. It normalized my struggle. My classification moved from spiritual loser to ordinary Christian, joining countless other believers who have endured the 'dark night of the soul' (see Psa. 22; 77; 88). I was released from what Packer calls 'a cruel treadmill life of hunting each day for non-existent failures in consecration.'[12] And it started me on the path of understanding the Christian life as warfare; of understanding the continuing problem of 'indwelling sin' in believers; of understanding the incompleteness of redemption in this world; of understanding our active participation in sanctification; of understanding our absolute dependence upon the Holy Spirit; and of understanding God's gracious purpose in refining us through our trials and tribulations.

There is nothing easy about the Christian life. We have a *world* that hates and persecutes us (John 15:18-25). We must deal with a *devil* who is a roaring lion seeking to devour us (1 Pet. 5:8). We have our own *flesh*, our own sinful inclination which wars against the Spirit, 'For the desires of the flesh are against the Spirit, and the desires of the Spirit are

---

[10] Owen, *Mortification*, 14.

[11] The phrase is that of Isaac Watts, 'Am I a Soldier of the Cross,' *Trinity Hymnal,* #573, stanza 2.

[12] Packer, *Knowing God*, 225.

against the flesh, for these are opposed to each other, to *keep you from doing the things you want to do*' (Gal. 5:17; 1 Pet. 2:11). Consequently the Christian life, says Warfield of the Protestant Reformers' view, is 'a life of continuous dissatisfaction with self.' Yet it is a life of joy found in a 'continuous looking afresh to Christ as the ground of all our hope.'[13]

Far from struggle being a sign of a defective Christian life, the absence of struggle may raise questions about the character of one's Christian experience. Why is the devil leaving you alone? Why has the world befriended you? Why are you not more troubled by your own flesh? Why are you not wrestling with 'the spiritual forces of evil in the heavenly places,' and deflecting the 'flaming darts of the evil one' (Eph. 6:12, 16)? Thankfully, Reformed Protestantism has had a firm grasp of the theme of the Christian's struggle. William Gurnall wrote over 1,100 pages of very small, double-column type on Christian warfare entitled *The Christian in Complete Armour*, and over three hundred years later Martyn Lloyd-Jones (1899–1981) published in two volumes *The Christian Warfare* and *The Christian Soldier,* totalling over 700 pages.[14] Both men were expounding Ephesians 6:10-20. Lloyd-Jones writes a wonderful chapter

---

[13] Warfield, *Perfectionism*, I:90. He continues: 'The more dissatisfaction we feel with ourselves, the more the greatness of Christ's salvation is manifest to us, and the more our delight in it waxes.'

[14] Martyn Lloyd-Jones, *The Christian Warfare* (Edinburgh: Banner of Truth Trust, 1976) and *The Christian Soldier* (Edinburgh: Banner of Truth Trust, 1977).

in *Christian Soldier* entitled 'Who Does the Fighting?' We do, of course, with the strength which God supplies. 'The state of grace,' says Gurnall, 'is the commencing of a war against sin, not the ending of it.'[15] We are called, he says, 'to proclaim and prosecute an irreconcilable war against (our) bosom sins.'[16] 'The Christian's life,' he maintains, 'is a continual wrestling.'[17]

[15] Gurnall, *Christian in Complete Armour*, I:121.
[16] *Ibid.*, I:13.
[17] *Ibid.*, I:114.

12

The Power

JOHN 15:5

I am the vine; you are the branches. Whoever abides in me and I in him, he it is that bears much fruit, for apart from me you can do nothing.

THE Christian life is a fight of faith (1 Tim. 6:12; 2 Tim. 4:7). In this fight we *struggle* (Col. 1:27). We *toil* and *strive* (1 Tim. 4:10). We *mortify* the flesh and *pursue* holiness (Rom. 8:13; Heb. 12:14). God gives us weapons and armour for the battle, yet we must do the *fighting* (2 Cor. 10:4; Eph. 6:10-20). The devil schemes against us (2 Cor. 2:11) and tempts us (1 Thess. 3:5). The world and its various lusts seek to entice and seduce us (1 John 2:15-17). Our own fleshly passions— the remnants of our fallen nature—'wage war' against our souls (1 Pet. 2:11; Rom. 7:23). These things are true of *all* of us who are believers. Not one of us is exempt.

Yet, for each one of us the battle differs. There are common features, yet because of our differing temperaments, because of our differing strengths and weaknesses, even differing strengths which become weaknesses, each of us faces distinctive struggles. Though freed from the bondage of sin (Rom. 6), we continue to wrestle with the remnants of sin (Rom. 7). For some, the struggle is with their fears, their anxieties, and their insecurities. They struggle to trust God on airplanes and highways, in storms and scary neighbourhoods, and with the safety and health of their children and spouses. They are white-knuckled the entire time they are aboard an airplane. They are ducking as eighteen-wheelers blow by on the interstates. They are paralyzed by their fears.

Others struggle with depression. They have no trouble with skydiving. Scuba-diving with the great whites? No problem. Fear is not an issue. Yet they are plunged into dark emotional places by unanticipated events which disrupt their lives, or failure in some attempted endeavour. They become distraught over a cross word from their employer, or a hostile look from a rival, or an argument with a family member. Some others struggle with chemical addictions, with alcohol and/or drugs. These are an enormous temptation for them. Another person struggles with the need for the approval of others, for popularity or recognition. They wouldn't dream of abusing drugs or alcohol. However, they are people-pleasers. They are tempted to compromise the gospel in order to protect a favourable image with the people who count.

Still others struggle with the allurements of immoral sensual pleasure. They are sorely tempted, even tortured, by pornography and sexual sin. Yet others who live morally straight and upright lives are not tempted at all by fleshly sins. They are tempted by pride and self-righteousness and judgmentalism. They struggle with Pharisaism. For some people it's food. How they struggle with overeating! For some it's material things. They can't resist shopping and buying all the pretty things they see or the neat gadgets and expensive toys they find in store windows, on the internet, or in catalogues. For still others, it is their runaway tongues, spewing criticism, cynicism, and gossip. It's a great weakness. They struggle to control their speech; still others struggle with anger, jealousy, covetousness, and envy.

The list could go on and on. We all struggle. Yes, our bondage to these sins has been broken. We have been born again (John 3:3ff.). We are new creatures in Christ. All things have been made new (2 Cor. 5:17). We are no longer *controlled by our sin*, but we do continue to fight with the *dregs of sin* remaining within us. Because I have victory in an area in which others struggle does not allow me to consider myself superior to them. Their temptation is not mine. My struggle is not theirs. Yet we are all tempted, we all stumble and fail, and we all long for victory.

Yet, 'thanks be to God,' says the apostle, 'who gives us the *victory* through the Lord Jesus Christ' (1 Cor. 15:57). We 'are *more than conquerors* through him who loved us' (Rom. 8:37). How do we enter into that victory? We must certainly strain like athletes and fight like warriors. However, of itself our personal effort is insufficient. Those who paid close attention in the last chapter will know this. Still, there may be some who were confused, even misled by our emphasis.

True vine

A crucial verse in my experience has been John 15:5. Jesus the True Vine says simply, 'Apart from me you can do nothing.' I can't say exactly when its impact was first felt, but it was very early on. Its truth led me during my college years to bury myself in my fraternity's windowless chapter-room reading Scripture and praying for an hour and a half before venturing out onto fraternity and sorority row on the way to campus. Suffice it to say that over the decades it has been my go-to verse for understanding my absolute incapacity for any spiritual good and my absolute dependence on Christ. The vine was a well-established Old Testament metaphor for Israel (Psa. 80:9-16; Isa. 5:1-7; Jer. 12:10ff.; Ezek. 15:1-8; Hos. 10:1, 2). Jesus, by applying the image of the vine to himself, distinguishing himself as the 'true' vine from Israel the failing and fruitless vine, is identifying himself as the true Israel, the one who will bear the intended fruit for God (John 15:1).

Consequently, he is the only one in connection with whom the people of God may live and bear fruit for God. We, his disciples, are but *branches*. 'I am the vine; you are the *branches*' (John 15:5; cf. verses 2, 4).

> As the branch cannot bear fruit by itself, unless it abides in the vine, neither can you, unless you abide in me (John 15:4).

As branches we have no capacity for life or fruitfulness apart from him. A 'branch cannot bear fruit by itself.' Our dependence is absolute. If severed from the vine, we become lifeless, fruitless and worthless. 'The bud of a good desire, the blossom of a good resolution, and the fruit of a good action, all come from him,' says John Trapp.[1] Jesus repeats the same again:

> I am the vine; you are the branches. Whoever abides in me and I in him, he it is that bears much fruit, for apart from me you can do nothing (John 15:5).

As branches we can only bear fruit in connection with the vine. Yet through union with the vine we can bear not just some, but 'much fruit.' The 'whole secret of the branch's life, strength, vigour, beauty, and fertility,' is in the vine, explains J. C. Ryle. Apart from the vine, we 'can do nothing.' 'Separate from the parent stem, the branch has no life of its own,' Ryle adds.[2] Our incapacity is absolute. The older commentators see the implications of Jesus' words with helpful clarity. 'We can do nothing towards our justification,' says Matthew Henry, 'and ... nothing towards our sanctification.' Apart from Christ, Henry continues, 'We can do nothing aright, nothing that will be fruit pleasing to God or profitable to ourselves.'[3] Apart from the True Vine, David Brown agrees, we can do 'nothing spiritually good, nothing which God

---

[1] Trapp, *Commentary*, V:397.
[2] J. C. Ryle, *Expository Thoughts, John*, III:71.
[3] Matthew Henry, *Exposition*, John 15:5.

will regard and accept as good.'[4] Only as we 'abide' in Christ, Jesus teaches, only as we remain in vital connection to him, drawing life and strength from him, do we live and bear fruit (John 15:6-9).

Faith unites us to Christ. We were buried with him in baptism and raised up with him in newness of life (Rom. 6:3ff.). He imparts to believers his Helper, the Holy Spirit (John 14:16, 17, 26). 'I will send to you … the Spirit of Truth,' who bears witness to the truth, convicts the world of the truth, and guides believers into 'all truth' (John 15:26; 16:7-15). The Spirit is Christ's gift to us. The Holy Spirit is 'the Spirit of Christ,' or 'the Spirit of Jesus' (Acts 16:7; Rom. 8:9; 1 Pet. 1:11). By the Spirit Christ himself comes to dwell in our hearts (John 14:20; Eph. 3:16, 17). By the Spirit Christ imparts his strength and perfects his power in all who recognize their weakness and depend upon his strength (2 Cor. 12:9, 10). There are two directions in which this vital lesson must be learned and applied: the Christian life and Christian ministry.

Christian life

We cannot of ourselves live the Christian life. We cannot do it on our own. Can we keep the commandments? No. Can we love our neighbours? No. Can we develop virtuous character? No. Yet we are born again, aren't we? Yes, I trust that we are. However, even with a new nature we can

---

[4] Brown, *The Four Gospels*, 440.

only conform with the perfect will of God imperfectly, and then only by the ongoing strength that he provides. Even the regenerate, even those who are true disciples of Christ, can only live the Christian life by the constant power that the True Vine supplies by his word and Spirit.

We may return to a number of passages we cited last time, now emphasizing not the human exertion side but the divine strength side of the Christian life. We may begin with Romans 8:13.

> *For if you live according to the flesh you will die, but if by the Spirit you put to death the deeds of the body, you will live.*

How are the 'deeds of the body' mortified or 'put to death'? It is only 'by the Spirit.' We are incapable of mortifying the flesh in our own strength. It is only by the power, by the strength, by the supernatural enabling of the Holy Spirit that we are able to defeat sin. We may return to Philippians 2:12, 13.

> *Therefore, my beloved, as you have always obeyed, so now, not only as in my presence but much more in my absence, work out your own salvation with fear and trembling, for it is God who works in you, both to will and to work for his good pleasure.*

In light of what Christ has done and shall do (Phil. 2:6-11), 'work out your own salvation with fear and trembling.' How can *I* do that? I am so weak and foolish. I am

[153]

so conflicted and compromised. How can I 'work out my salvation'? We only are able to work out the matters of our salvation, our sanctification and growth, our faith and obedience, our perseverance and preservation, because 'it is God who works' in us, enabling us 'both to will and to work for his good pleasure'; that is, both to want, to desire, and to achieve that which pleases God. The 'will' to do what pleases God and 'work' itself that pleases him requires what the Scot James Fergusson (1621–67) calls 'a pull of omnipotent power.'[5] We are incapable of this on our own. We can't maintain the disciplines of the Christian life (prayer, Scripture study/meditation, public devotion, family devotion), or the pattern of obedience, or a life of holiness, or a life of sacrificial love and service, or constancy in the midst of persecution and suffering. We can't do it except as Christ enables by his own work. We may return to Ephesians 6:10-13.

> *Finally, be strong in the Lord and in the strength of his might. Put on the whole armour of God, that you may be able to stand against the schemes of the devil. For we do not wrestle against flesh and blood, but against the rulers, against the authorities, against the cosmic powers over this present darkness, against the spiritual forces of evil in the heavenly places. Therefore take up the whole armour of*

[5] James Fergusson and David Dickson, *The Epistles of Paul to the Galatians, Ephesians, Philippians, Colossians, Thessalonians, and Hebrews, Geneva Series Commentary* (1656–74; 1841; repr. Edinburgh: Banner of Truth Trust, 1978), 300.

God, that you may be able to withstand in the evil day, and
having done all, to stand firm.

Note the unequal contest. We are up against a schem-
ing devil, no less. We do not fight against 'flesh and blood,'
ordinary human beings, but 'cosmic powers,' the 'present
darkness' over which they rule, even 'the spiritual forces of
evil in the heavenly places.' How can we do this? He urges
us to 'be strong.' The problem is that they are strong and we
comparatively are weak. We only can 'be strong *in the Lord.*'
We only can be strong 'in the strength of *his* might.' The
armour that we put on is 'the whole,' the comprehensive,
the complete 'armour *of God*,' that covers every vulnerabil-
ity. 'God is the author, maker, and inventor of this armour,'
says Fergusson.[6] Only with God's armour are we 'able to
withstand in the evil day,' and to 'stand firm.' Only with the
shield that he provides are we able to extinguish the 'flaming
darts of the evil one' (Eph. 6:16). *Never* could we stand and
fight in our own strength. Our dependence is absolute.

We believers desire to grow in Christ-likeness. We want
to grow in love, peace, patience, kindness, faithfulness, and
self-control. We long to be characterized by these and other
virtues. How may this come about? Can we produce these
virtues by our own moral efforts? Can we generate them
by exceptional exertions? Is it merely a matter of sufficient
natural discipline? Of course not. These virtues are the 'fruit
of the Spirit' (Gal. 5:22-24). We manifest the fruit. We come

[6] *Ibid.,* 261.

to be characterized by the fruit. However, the Holy Spirit produces them. They are *his* fruit, produced by *his* power.

Christian ministry

We see our dependence on Jesus the True Vine in connection with fruitful 'ministry' as well, whether of the official and ordained sort, or the informal ordinary member sort. We shall have much more to say about the ministry in another book in this series. For now, we affirm that we cannot serve Christ faithfully or fruitfully apart from strength, the gifts, the capacities and opportunities that Christ supplies through his Spirit. How did the apostle Paul become a minister of the gospel? By 'the gift of God's grace' and 'the working of his power' (Eph. 3:7). Both in terms of initiation and continuation of his ministry, the apostle was dependent upon God's grace and power. He affirms this repeatedly.

> *For this I toil, struggling with all his energy that he power-fully works within me* (Col. 1:29).

The apostle is toiling and struggling in the ministry of proclaiming Christ in such a way 'that we may present everyone mature in Christ' (Col. 1:28). Does he do this in his own natural strength? Is he limited to his own natural ability? If he were, nothing would come of it. No, he labours 'with all *his* energy that *he* powerfully works within me.' 'He did this,' says the Puritan commentator John Davenant (1572–1641), 'not relying upon human strength or his own powers, but upon the divine assistance of Christ, strengthened and aided by his might.'[7] The apostle is only able to minster powerfully because of the powerful Spirit of Christ imparting his power. The apostle cannot faithfully and fruitfully minister on his own.

We see this again as the apostle describes his own ministry:

> *But by the grace of God I am what I am, and his grace toward me was not in vain. On the contrary, I worked harder than any of them, though it was not I, but the grace of God that is with me* (1 Cor. 15:10).

His initial statement sums it all up. It is only 'by the grace of God' that he is what he is: both saved and serving. He can honestly say, 'I worked harder than any of them.' Humanly speaking this was true. Compared with the labour of others, he worked hardest of all. Yet he cannot take credit for this. Why not? Because '*it was not I*, but the grace of God that is with me.' He had no personal or natural capacity even to work hard, never mind fruitfully, or faithfully, apart from strength that Christ supplies through his Spirit. Speaking of his wider, collegial ministry, he writes:

> *What then is Apollos? What is Paul? Servants through whom you believed, as the Lord assigned to each. I planted, Apollos watered, but God gave the growth* (1 Cor. 3:5, 6).

---

[7] John Davenant, *Colossians*: A Geneva Series Commentary, Vols. I & II (1627, 1831; repr. Edinburgh: Banner of Truth Trust, 2005), I:329.

The newly converted Philip Melanchthon (1497–1560), Luther's most trusted assistant, thought it impossible that his listeners could fail to understand the case for the gospel of grace which he had found so compelling. Before long he was heard to say that the old Adam was too hard for the young Melanchthon. Only by the power of the Spirit can we enjoy fruitful ministry. Paul and Apollos worked. They planted and watered. They laboured hard. Farming or even gardening is difficult, strenuous work. However, all the fruit of their effort was God's. '*God* gave the growth.' 'Success' in ministry is in God's hands and of his doing.

Consider Romans 12:1, 2:

> *I appeal to you therefore, brothers, by the mercies of God, to present your bodies as a living sacrifice, holy and acceptable to God, which is your spiritual worship. Do not be conformed to this world, but be transformed by the renewal of your mind, that by testing you may discern what is the will of God, what is good and acceptable and perfect.*

How are we able to give ourselves over to God in the totality of our being, body and soul, as a 'living sacrifice,' as an act of 'spiritual worship' or 'spiritual service of worship' (NASB)? This is not a natural desire. I want to live my own life, not place it on an altar of sacrifice. I have my own ambitions and dreams which I long to preserve. I would rather serve myself than God and others. It is only 'by the mercies of God,' understood and received, that I am enabled to present my body as a 'living sacrifice.' Only by his mercy will we avoid conformity with the world, will we be transformed, will our minds be renewed, will we discern what the 'good and acceptable and perfect' will of God is, and offer ourselves for service.

How can we minister today? How can we—with all the challenges we face from a hostile, modern, secular, relativistic world? Only by the supernatural 'gifts of the Spirit' described in 1 Corinthians 12, Romans 12, and Ephesians 4. We minister not merely with natural gifts, though these play a part. Rather, the Holy Spirit must empower our ministry if it is to be faithful and fruitful. We all are '*empowered* by one and the same Spirit, who apportions to each one individually as he wills,' the apostle teaches us (1 Cor. 12:11). We cannot serve Christ faithfully and fruitfully in our own strength. He must empower. He must enable. He must impart his spiritual gifts or our labour is futile.

'Who is sufficient for these things?' the apostle asks (2 Cor. 2:16). 'Our sufficiency is *from God who has made us sufficient* to be ministers of a new covenant, not of the letter but of the Spirit' (2 Cor. 3:5, 6). *He* makes us sufficient. Indeed, 'I can do all things,' live a life of faithful obedience, minister in all places and under all conditions, not in my own strength or my own wisdom, but '*through him who strengthens me*' (Phil. 4:13).

13

Accessing the Power

2 TIMOTHY 3:16, 17

All Scripture is breathed out by God and profitable for teaching, for reproof, for correction, and for training in righteousness, that the man of God may be complete, equipped for every good work.

THIRTEEN Christian missionaries and their children were brutally massacred in Zimbabwe in June, 1978. Their murderers bayoneted them to death, and mutilated their bodies, which were thrown into the bush for the elements and scavengers to consume. One of these missionaries, Wendy White, the friend of a friend of a friend of ours, called out as she died, 'Fear not those who will kill the body—they cannot kill the soul.'[1]

In 1967 a teenage girl dove into the shallow waters of the Chesapeake Bay, breaking her neck and becoming

---

[1] Cited in Faith Cook, *And So I Began to Read: Books That Have Influenced Me* (Welwyn Garden City: Evangelical Press Books, 2006), 41.

a quadriplegic, paralyzed from the shoulders down. For months she wanted only to die. Eventually she was reconciled to God's purposes for her. At the time of her accident she was a believer. However, Joni Eareckson Tada says that her immature faith 'confused the abundant Christian life with the great American dream: I was a Christian and would … marry a wonderful man who made $250,000 a year, and we'd have 2.5 children. It was me-focused: What can God do for me?' Today she reflects: 'Had I not broken my neck I'd probably be on my second divorce, maxing out on my husband's credit cards, planning my next ski vacation. I wouldn't be here extolling the glories of the gospel and the power of God to help a person smile, not in spite of the problems, but because of them.'[2]

How can we come to have the kind of courageous faith exemplified by these two women? How can we live and serve faithfully and fruitfully? Jesus gave to the disciples the key just prior to his Ascension:

> *You are witnesses of these things. And behold, I am sending the promise of my Father upon you. But stay in the city until you are clothed with power from on high* (Luke 24:48, 49).

How could these fearful, mainly uneducated, common men be 'witnesses' for Christ to the nations? Not in their own strength and will. They must be 'clothed with power from on high.' Again Jesus said to them,

[2] Marvin Olasky, 'July 4, 10, 30, 31: Connecting the Dots and Beating Depression,' *World Magazine*, August 5, 2017, 64.

But you will receive power when the Holy Spirit has come upon you, and you will be my witnesses in Jerusalem and in all Judea and Samaria, and to the end of the earth (Acts 1:8).

The promise is 'power' for ministry. Only with Holy Spirit power—Pentecost power—could they be faithful in life and fruitful in witness 'to the end of the earth.' The Holy Spirit, says John Davenant, is 'the fountain and the principle of all might and spiritual strength.'[3] Apart from the True Vine we can do nothing (John 15:5). Only as the Spirit unites us to Christ shall we be supplied with the power we need to live the Christian life. As John the Baptist said, 'A person cannot receive even one thing unless it is given him from heaven' (John 3:27). Our dependence is absolute. Consequently, we wish to understand two crucial lessons. First, who is the Holy Spirit? Second, how do you go about accessing his power?

Holy Spirit

The church in which I was reared was evangelical and Bible-believing. The gospel was preached every Sunday. I was in church every Sunday. Yet in all those years I cannot recall a single sermon about the Holy Spirit. To be fair, the role of the Spirit surely must have been included in those pulpit messages. We certainly heard almost weekly about being 'born again' (John 4:1-4, 7). Yet that was never related to

---

[3] Davenant, *Colossians*, p. 330, on Col. 1:29.

being 'born *of the Spirit*' (John 4:5, 6, 8). It could be that what was taught I simply did not hear. Yet it remains the case that I can't remember a single mention, never mind a single message on the Holy Spirit.

While in college I was introduced to Ephesians 5:18: 'And do not get drunk with wine, for that is debauchery, but be filled with the Spirit.' A little booklet produced by Campus Crusade ('the bird book' mentioned earlier) taught us how to be 'filled with the Spirit.' Its presentation of 'spiritual breathing' was too mechanical and simplistic to be of enduring help. Yet because it was my first introduction to being 'filled,' that is, controlled by, under the influence of, even under the direction of the Holy Spirit, it was a breakthrough for me in understanding the Christian life. Up to that point I had been like John the Baptist's disciples at Ephesus who admitted to the apostle Paul that 'we have not even heard that there is a Holy Spirit' (Acts 19:2). The impression I had as a young Christian was that until Campus Crusade's work in the mid-1960s on one hand, and on the other hand until the Jesus Movement in Southern California in the late 1960s and early 1970s with its charismatic emphasis, the Holy Spirit had been unknown or at least long neglected. Only much later did I discover that the Spirit's vital role in our salvation was well understood by previous generations.

Historic doctrine

What does the Bible teach and what has the church believed about the Holy Spirit? What is the historic, orthodox, catholic, and reformed doctrine? The ancient Nicene Creed outlines several basic elements.

> And we believe in the Holy Spirit, the Lord and giver of life, who proceeds from the Father and the Son; who with the Father and the Son together is worshipped and glorified; who spoke by the prophets …

First, he is the third person of the Trinity in whom we are to believe, who is of one substance or essence with the Father and the Son, and is equal in power and eternity.

Second, he 'proceeds from the Father and the Son' (John 16:7).[4]

Third, he is to be 'worshipped and glorified' along with the Father and the Son.

Fourth, he 'spoke by the prophets.' By his agency we have the Holy Scriptures as 'men spoke from God as they were carried along by the Holy Spirit' (2 Pet. 1:21).

Fifth, and most important for our purposes in this study, he is redemption's agent of the application. He is 'the Lord and giver of life,' both physical and spiritual. It was Calvin's profound understanding of this fifth item that earned him

---

[4] This, the *filioque* clause 'and the Son,' was hotly disputed in the church of late antiquity and into the Middle Ages and was a major factor in the division of the Western (Catholic) and Eastern (Orthodox) churches in 1054.

the title of 'the theologian of the Holy Spirit,' as Warfield insisted he should be known.[5] Calvin replaced the church with the Holy Spirit as the immediate agent of application. The 'proper work' of the Spirit, says Calvin, 'is to make us partakers not only of Christ himself, but of all his blessings.'[6] The Puritans gave great emphasis to the work of the Spirit, the emphatic evidence of which might perhaps be John Owen's massive, carefully argued, brilliantly illuminating 651-page *Discourse Concerning the Holy Spirit.*[7] His successors include George Smeaton (1814–89), Abraham Kuyper (1837–1920), and Sinclair B. Ferguson, each of whom have written significant expositions on the person and work of the Holy Spirit.[8] No, the Holy Spirit was not discovered by Campus Crusade and the Charismatics in California in the 1960s.

The Reformed church often has utilized this simple formula:

---

[5] B. B. Warfield, *Calvin and Augustine* (Philadelphia: Presbyterian and Reformed Publishing Co., 1956), 485.

[6] John Calvin, *The Gospel According to St John*: 11-21, Calvin's Commentaries translated by T. H. L. Parker; edited by David W. and Thomas F. Torrance (Grand Rapids: William B. Eerdmans Publishing, 1959), 82.

[7] John Owen, 'Discourse Concerning the Holy Spirit,' *The Works of John Owen*, Volumes I-XVI. 1674, 1850–53; repr. London: Banner of Truth Trust, 1965), Vol. III.

[8] George Smeaton, *The Doctrine of the Holy Spirit* (1882; repr. Edinburgh: Banner of Truth Trust, 2016); Abraham Kuyper, *The Work of the Holy Spirit*, translated by Henry de Vries (1900; repr. New York: Cosimo, Inc., 2007); Sinclair B. Ferguson, *The Holy Spirit*, Contours of Christian Theology (Downers Grove, IL: InterVarsity Press, 1996).

What the Father *planned,* the Son *accomplished,* and the Holy Spirit *applies.*

Salvation is a Trinitarian work. Indeed, it is true to say that the Trinity was fully revealed only in the context of redemption. This is particularly true of the Holy Spirit, especially with regard to his deity and distinctive personhood. Owen writes,

> There was no more glorious mystery brought to light in and by Jesus Christ than that of the holy Trinity, or the subsistence of the three persons in the unity of the same divine nature.[9]

The Holy Spirit was at work in the Old Testament, yet that work was particular and periodic, empowering some, not all, at times, not always.[10] However, the Hebrew prophets promised that in the age to come the Spirit would rest upon the Messiah (Isa. 11:2; 42:1; 48:16; 61:1) and upon the

---

[9] Owen, 'Holy Spirit,' *Works*, III:158.

[10] Bezaleel and those who were to be engaged in constructing the tabernacle and all its furnishings were 'filled with the Spirit of God, with ability and intelligence, with knowledge and all craftsmanship' (Exod. 31:3; cf. 35:31). We see the Spirit of God upon Moses (Num. 11:17), the seventy elders (Num. 11:25), Joshua (Num. 27:18), Balaam (Num. 24:2), Othniel (Judg. 3:10), Gideon (Judg. 6:34), Jephthah (Judg. 11:29), Samson (Judg. 13:25; 14:6, 19; 15:14), Saul (1 Sam. 10:6, 10; 11:6; 16:14; 19:23), David (1 Sam. 16:13; 2 Sam. 23:2; cf. Psa. 51:11; 143:10), Saul's messengers (1 Sam. 19:20), Amasai (1 Chron. 12:18), Azariah (2 Chron. 15:1), Zedekiah (2 Chron. 18:23), Jahaziel (2 Chron. 20:14), Zechariah (2 Chron. 24:20), Isaiah (Isa. 61:1), Ezekiel (Ezek. 2:2; 3:24; 8:3; 11:1, 5, 24, etc.), and perhaps Daniel (Dan. 4:18, etc.) and all the prophets (Neh. 9:30; Zech. 12:1).

whole people of God (Isa. 32:15; 34:16; 44:3; 59:21; Ezek. 11:19; 36:26, 27; 37:14; 39:29; Joel 2:28, 29; Zech. 4:6). The Spirit's identity and work only came to fruition in the New Testament.

The historic Reformed view of the particular role of the Holy Spirit is reflected in the *Shorter Catechism*:

> Q. 29. How are we made partakers of the redemption purchased by Christ?
> A. We are made partakers of the redemption purchased by Christ, by the effectual application of it to us by his Holy Spirit.[11]

The *application* of the benefits of that work, eternally *planned* by the Father, *accomplished* by the Son, is the role of the Holy Spirit.[12]

---

[11] *Shorter Catechism* Question 20 speaks of God's (*i.e.*, the Father's) eternal determination to deliver humanity out of its sin and misery by a redeemer. That redeemer, Jesus Christ, 'purchased' redemption.

[12] While affirming the distinctive work of the Holy Spirit, we are not denying the principle of *opera Trinitatis ad extra sunt indivisa*, that each person of the Trinity is active in the work of the one person so that in all the external works of the Trinity the three persons are undivided. Their shared essence, indeed their unity as one God, means that they share in all the works of the Godhead. The distinction in persons means that they each have their particular tasks. Augustine, commenting on John 14:10, affirms that 'the attributes of the three are inseparable, so that when an activity is attributed to the Father, he is not to be engaged in it without the Son and the Holy Spirit. And when it is of an activity of the Son, it is not without the Father and the Holy Spirit. And when it is an activity of the Spirit, it is not without the Father and the Son' (Augustine, cited in *Ancient Christian Commentary on Scripture*, Joel C. Elowsky, ed. Downers Grove, IL: InterVarsity Press, 2006, IVb:133).

We may put the matter as follows:

The events of the cross occurred two thousand years ago. From an American perspective, they took place all the way across the Atlantic Ocean, across the whole length of the Mediterranean Sea, in Palestine. How do those benefits pass through all that time and all that space? The answer is, the Holy Spirit works in conjunction with the word (in its various forms: read, prayed, sung, displayed, and especially, preached) to bring those benefits to us. The *Shorter Catechism* summarizes the historic Reformed view for us.

> Q. 89. How is the word made effectual to salvation?
> A. The Spirit of God makes the reading, but especially the preaching of the word, an effectual means of convincing and converting sinners, and of building them up in holiness and comfort, through faith, unto salvation (cf. *Larger Catechism*, Q.&A. 155).

The Spirit works through the word to save and sanctify. He empowers the gospel-word of Christ (again, John 15:26; 16:13-15). The sword of the Spirit is the word of God (Eph. 6:17). The Spirit is received 'by hearing [the gospel] with faith' (Gal. 3:2).

Through the word the whole *ordo salutis* (order of salvation) is applied by the Spirit to believers. Those who are born again are born of the Spirit (John 3:3, 6, 8). Those who believe receive faith as a gift of God (Eph. 2:8, 9). Sanctification is the fruit of the presence of the Spirit in one's life (Gal. 5:16-18, 22-24); 'sanctification' is 'of the Spirit'

(1 Pet. 1:2). The Spirit is the 'Spirit of adoption' (Rom. 8:15, 16; cf. Gal. 4:4-7). The Spirit 'seals' or secures and preserves believers for the completion of our redemption (Eph. 4:30). He is the 'guarantee' of their future glory (Eph. 1:13; 2 Cor. 1:22). The entire *ordo* from regeneration to glorification is the Spirit's work. Again we cite Owen:

> There is not any spiritual or *saving good* from first to last, communicated unto us, or that we are from and by the grace of God made partakers of, but it is revealed to us and bestowed on us by the Holy Ghost.[13]

The whole Christian life, we learn from Galatians 5, is a matter of '*walking* by the Spirit' (Gal. 5:16); being *led* by the Spirit (Gal. 5:25); and *keeping in step* with the Spirit (Gal. 5:25). We learn the same in Romans 8 (as we will see). The whole Christian life, from rebirth to glory is enabled by the Holy Spirit. What I did not understand as a child of the church about the vital role of the Holy Spirit must be understood if believers are to thrive spiritually.

Accessing the power

The question that remains is this: How do we go about *accessing* this divine strength for life and ministry? We have

---

[13] Owen, 'Holy Spirit,' *Works*, III:27. Jesus teaches that apart from him we can do nothing (John 15:5). Yet by the Holy Spirit alone, we are able to 'abide in Christ,' says Owen, and by the Spirit alone 'is the grace of Christ communicated unto us and wrought in us.' To what extent is this true? Owen answers, 'By him we are *regenerated*; by him we are *sanctified*; by him are we *assisted* in and unto every good work.'

nothing new to say here. We access God's strength through what sometimes is referred to as God's *ordinances,* more frequently the *ordinary means of grace,* that is, the word, sacraments, and prayer as they are administered publicly, privately, and in families.[14] The *Shorter Catechism* may once again summarize the historic Reformed view:

> Q. 88. What are the outward and ordinary means whereby Christ communicateth to us the benefits of redemption?
> A. The outward and ordinary means whereby Christ communicateth to us the benefits of redemption are, his ordinances, especially the word, sacraments, and prayer; all which are made effectual to the elect for salvation (cf. *Larger Catechism* Q.&A. 154).

The Holy Spirit working through the word takes what Christ has accomplished and applies it to us today. 2 Timothy 3:15-17 has played a vital role in building my confidence in the power of God's word, and then by extension, in prayer as well, as the means by which we are able faithfully and fruitfully to live the Christian life and minister Christ's gospel.

---

[14] For the use of *ordinance(s)* to indicate the primary means of grace, see *Westminster Confession of Faith* XXVIII.5, 6; XXIV.3, 7; *Shorter Catechism,* Questions 50, 54, 88, 92; *Larger Catechism,* Questions 108, 109, 113, 154, 162, 174, 175, and perhaps 190, 191.

Word

> ... *from childhood you have been acquainted with the sacred writings, which are able to make you wise for salvation through faith in Christ Jesus. All Scripture is breathed out by God and profitable for teaching, for reproof, for correction, and for training in righteousness, that the man of God may be complete, equipped for every good work* (2 Tim. 3:15-17).

God's word, written, spoken, and displayed in the church's administration of the sacraments, as empowered by the Holy Spirit, is 'able to make [us] wise for salvation through faith in Jesus Christ' (verse 15). The Scriptures have this capacity. They have this power to make us wise. They are able to teach, reprove, correct, and train us (verse 16). By the Scriptures believers are 'equipped for every good work'—not some, not most, but all, even *every* good work (verses 16, 17). They have the power, the capacity to equip. Jesus prays that we be sanctified 'in the truth.' The truth has that capacity (John 17:17). It has sanctifying power. The gospel is 'the *power* of God for salvation' (Rom. 1:16). It has the *power* to regenerate, convert, and impart justifying faith. The word of God comes to us 'not only in word, but also in *power* and in the Holy Spirit and with full conviction' (1 Thess. 1:5). Don't think of the word as merely mental or intellectual information. Don't disparage Bible knowledge as mere 'head knowledge.' The word, the apostle tells us, 'is *at work* in you believers' (1 Thess. 2:13). The word has this working, effectual power. We grow by 'the pure milk of the word.' It is 'by it,' by the transformative power of the word, that we 'grow in respect to salvation' (1 Pet. 2:1, 2, NASB).

The 'blessed man' of Psalm 1 is one whose

> delight is in the law of the LORD,
>   and on his law he meditates day and night.
> He is like a tree planted by streams of water
>   that yields its fruit in its season,
>   and its leaf does not wither.
> In all that he does, he prospers (Psa. 1:2, 3).

The psalmist likens the word of God to a refreshing, nourishing, growth-inducing stream of water. Those who meditate on the law (*torah*), the fatherly instruction of God, are like a tree—a metaphor of strength and stability—planted by that stream that 'yields its fruit in its season' and 'prospers' (Psa. 1:3). From the stream 'a good man receives supplies of strength and vigour,' says Matthew Henry. The word of God 'keeps him out of the way of the ungodly and fortifies him against their temptations.'[15] This healthy, fruitful, rooted, thriving tree is contrasted with 'chaff' which is light, weightless, and worthless (Psa. 1:4). The more we meditate on God's word ('day and night'), 'the better furnished we are for every good word and work,' Henry explains.[16] Devote yourself to personal Bible reading. Devote yourself to Bible meditation and memorization. Devote your family to reading Scripture together. Devote yourself to the public

---

[15] Henry, *Exposition,* on Psa. 1:3.
[16] *Ibid.*

preaching of God's word. Devote yourself to worship that not only preaches but reads, prays, and sings and displays (in the sacraments) God's powerful word. Want the power of God released in your life? Then 'read, mark, learn, and inwardly digest' God's word.

Prayer

Not only do we have the repeated promises of Jesus that if we pray, what we request will be given to us (Matt. 7:7-11; 18:19; 21:22; John 14:13; 15:7, 16; 16:23, 24; cf. 1 John 3:22; 5:14, 15), but we have the specific promise that if we ask for the Holy Spirit, he will be given to us.

> *If you then, who are evil, know how to give good gifts to your children, how much more will the heavenly Father give the Holy Spirit to those who ask him!* (Luke 11:13).

The presence of the Holy Spirit means *power*, as we've seen. This promise of Jesus, by the way, teaches us not only *whom* we are to seek in prayer (the Spirit), but *what* (spiritual realities) we are primarily to seek. Our congregation utilizes a weekly prayer list in which we place at the top what we call 'Spiritual Concerns.' Before we pray for current events, health concerns, or even the programme of the church, we pray for the spiritual condition of the church. We prioritize spiritual growth: victory over sin, the ripening fruit of the Spirit, greater holiness, a burden for lost souls, and so on. Why do we pray for these things? Because prayer is the means by which they become a reality in our experience. If we want the spiritual power by which to live the Christian life, we must ask for the Holy Spirit's presence and power. If we ask, seek and knock, it will be given to us, just as the Lord Jesus promised (Matt. 7:7-11). Yet we must ask.

The importance of prayer in strengthening the people of God can be seen both in the apostle's great prayers *for* the churches and his requests for prayer *from* the churches. Review Ephesians 1:16-23; 3:14-21; Colossians 1:9-14, and Philippians 1:9-11, as the apostle prays for his fellow disciples—for their wisdom, understanding, knowledge and discernment—all qualities which are vital for their spiritual well-being. He prays because he knows it is through prayer that God has promised to impart these virtues. To the Lord belongs 'wisdom and might,' and 'he gives wisdom to the wise and knowledge to those who have understanding' (see Dan. 2:20, 21). To what end? That they may see 'the immeasurable greatness of his power towards us who believe' (Eph. 1:19). What do they need? Power that is *immeasurably* great. To what end? To the end that,

> *according to the riches of his glory he may grant you to be strengthened with power through his Spirit in your inner being* (Eph. 3:16).

Believers need 'to be strengthened.' They need 'power.' By what means shall they acquire it? By the Spirit through the apostle's prayers.

To what end does he pray for 'knowledge,' wisdom,' and understanding'? To the end that they may—

walk in a manner worthy of the Lord, fully pleasing to him: bearing fruit in every good work and increasing in the knowledge of God; being strengthened with all power, according to his glorious might, for all endurance and patience with joy (Col. 1:10, 11).

His people need to be 'strengthened with all power, according to his glorious might,' enabling them to 'walk in a manner worthy of the Lord, fully pleasing to him' and 'bearing fruit.' Prayer is the means of bringing this about, of accessing God's power, resulting in a worthy Christian walk.

To what end does he pray for 'knowledge and all discernment?' (Phil. 1:9). To the end that they

may approve what is excellent, and so be pure and blameless for the day of Christ (Phil. 1:10; cf. Rom. 15:13; 2 Thess. 1:11, 12).

How do we come to make good decisions leading to good behaviour? How do we gain the capacity to 'approve what is excellent' so that we might be 'pure and blameless'? Through prayer. Prayer might not be the only factor. It may not be the most prominent factor in any given case. Yet it is a vital and irreplaceable ordinance by which the power of God for Christian living is accessed.

The apostle Paul not only prays for the churches, but also solicits the church's prayers. Not only does the apostle instruct the church to 'continue steadfastly in prayer,' but to 'pray also for us.' To what end? 'That God may open to us a door for the word.' Prayer opens doors. Prayer creates opportunities. Prayer changes things. Also, 'That I may make it clear, which is how I ought to speak' (Col. 4:2-4). The prayers of others enable the apostle to speak wisely and fruitfully (cf. Eph. 6:19; 2 Thess. 3:1, 2). Their prayers enable his acceptable service (Rom. 15:30). Their prayers result in his receiving help and blessing (2 Cor. 1:11; cf. Phil. 1:19). As the people of God 'draw near' to God's 'throne of grace' in prayer, they 'receive mercy and find grace to help in time of need' (Heb. 4:16). Will I be able to endure persecution? Will I be able to handle a death in the family or news of a crippling accident, or a bad report from a doctor? Will I have the strength to meet the challenges of life? Yes I will, if I access divine power through the word and prayer.

Final thoughts

We are meant to learn dependence, not for dependence's sake, but for survival's sake. We are not meant to learn dependence in order to perpetuate spiritual childhood, but to facilitate spiritual maturity. Dependence is necessary because spiritual reality requires it. In the natural realm, personal maturity, wisdom, and strength require increasing *independence*. Natural adulthood requires *self-sufficiency* and *decreasing dependence* on parents and other human relations. The opposite is true in the spiritual realm. The spiritual realm is more like the realm of flight. We don't fly by learning to flap our wings independently of all mechanical means. We are only able to fly when we face the reality of our dependence on machines. We only will remain airborne in a world ruled by the laws of gravity if we rely upon powerful aircraft. We cannot learn to breathe under water by sucking into our lungs water as though we had gills. We can only exist and thrive in a watery environment by depending on mechanical means. Learning dependence in the air or under water is vital. Learning dependence is also vital for finite beings who live in the environment of a fallen world, dominated as it is by the flesh and the devil. Maturity, wisdom, strength, and even life itself come only through increased dependence on their source in Christ, the True Vine.

Look again at Hebrews 12:1:

> *Therefore, since we are surrounded by so great a cloud of witnesses, let us also lay aside every weight, and sin which clings so closely, and let us run with endurance the race that is set before us…*

How are we to 'lay aside' our various entanglements and sins which cling to our souls? O how sin clings to us! We struggle to shake ourselves loose from it. How then can we 'run with endurance the race that is set before us?' Only by—

> *looking to Jesus, the founder and perfecter of our faith, who for the joy that was set before him endured the cross, despising the shame, and is seated at the right hand of the throne of God* (verse 2).

It is only as we look to Jesus for inspiration, for faith, for grace, for strength, and for power, that we are able to run the race. He is both 'a pattern' and 'a help,' says Matthew Poole. 'The disposition, grace, ability, and success which they have for running,' Poole continues, 'is *all from him*.'[17] He who is the 'founder' of our faith is also its 'perfecter.' Only as we look to him are we able to run the difficult race that is the Christian life.

Eric Liddell's (1902–45) most recent biographer has collected a number of testimonials about his character, so beautifully portrayed in the film *Chariots of Fire.* His principled refusal to compete in the 100 metres because the preliminaries heats were held on Sunday is well known. Less well known are his post-Olympics heroics.

Following his remarkable gold medal in the 400 metres track event at the Paris Olympics in 1924, Liddell returned to the mission field in China, the country in which he had been born to missionary parents. In 1943 his mission compound was overrun by the Japanese army and Liddell was taken into captivity. Living under the terrible conditions of an internment camp for almost the last two of years of his life, Liddell died of a brain tumour in 1945 at the age of 43.

Conditions in the camp were horrible. Food was scarce. The camp was infested with rats. Lice, mosquitoes, and flies tormented the internees. Disease was rampant. Conflict was common. In this dog-eat-dog, survival-of-the-fittest-world,

---

[17] Poole, *Commentary*, III:869 (emphasis added).

Liddell stood out. Here's what his fellow internees said about him:

> It is rare indeed when a person has the good fortune to meet a saint. He came as close to it as anyone I have ever known.[18]

They could not recall from him a single act of envy, pettiness, hubris, or self-aggrandizement. He 'became the camp's conscience without ever being pious, sanctimonious, or judgmental,' according to his biographer.[19] 'He was the consoling Samaritan of the camp, the epitome of a good neighbour.'[20] Internees remarked of his 'serene temper,' 'unruffled spirit' and 'constantly smiling face.' One regarded him as 'surely the most modest man who ever breathed.'[21] Still another said, 'He was always so positive—even when there wasn't much to be positive about, and he carried the weight of others' worries and burdens without hesitation.' Finally this—a diary entry of one of the internees at the time of Liddell's death:

> We confided in him, went to him for advice, looked on him as probably the most perfect and honourable Christian friend we had ever known, and the whole camp feels that in losing Eric they have lost a real friend.[22]

[18] Duncan Hamilton, *For the Glory: Eric Liddell's Journey from Olympic Champion to Modern Martyr* (New York: Penguin Press, 2016), 9.
[19] *Ibid.*, 8.
[20] *Ibid.*, 253.
[21] *Ibid.*, 257.
[22] *Ibid.*, 325.

Surely we all wish to become the sort of person who would attract such words of admiration.

How does it happen?

The gospel turns sinners into saints. It does so by the power of the Holy Spirit working through the ordinary means of the word of God (heard, read, and seen) and prayer.

Let us then access the power of God through his Spirit-empowered ordinances that we might become all that he calls us to be.

14

You Are Not Your Own

I CORINTHIANS 6:16-20

Or do you not know that he who is joined to a prostitute becomes one body with her? For, as it is written, 'The two will become one flesh.' But he who is joined to the Lord becomes one spirit with him. Flee from sexual immorality. Every other sin a person commits is outside the body, but the sexually immoral person sins against his own body. Or do you not know that your body is a temple of the Holy Spirit within you, whom you have from God? You are not your own, for you were bought with a price. So glorify God in your body.

SERMONS have always played a key role in my spiritual growth. Brother Canavan, the pastor of my childhood and youth, made an important impact on me through his evangelistic preaching. Pastor-teacher John MacArthur's preaching during my college years had a transformational impact week after week for months on end. Perhaps the greatest sermon

I've ever heard was delivered at the Banner of Truth Trust's annual ministers' conference in Leicester, England in the spring of 1979. I attended the conference with several fellow classmates from Trinity College in Bristol, also in England. The preacher was Al Martin, the pastor of Trinity Baptist Church, Montville, New Jersey, and his sermon was entitled 'Nothing but Christ Crucified,' an exposition of 1 Corinthians 2:2. I had not heard of Al Martin, so I came to that conference session blind, so to speak, and by the end of his message, given the volume of his vehemence, close to deaf!

Al Martin's sermon was absolutely overwhelming. It was overwhelming in every way.

For sheer volume, I had never in my twenty-four years heard anything so loud. I say this as one who grew up listening to vehement Baptist preachers. Those who sat in the front rows when he preached claimed he parted their hair. He preached with an urgency, I'm tempted to say ferocity, that astonished me. His voice would build over the course of a single sentence, beginning at a normal level and building to a fever pitch within a single breath.

What did he say that was so profound? Martin demonstrated in the front end of the sermon that every attribute of God comes to its ultimate expression at the cross. The justice of God? The wage of sin had to be paid if sinners were to be forgiven and reconciled to God (Rom. 6:23). God is just when he justifies (Rom. 3:26). The wrath of God? Look at the suffering of Christ. His sacrifice is one which propitiates, that puts away wrath (Rom. 3:25; 1 John 2:2). The love of God? Does it get any clearer than at the cross? 'God so loved the world that he gave his one and only Son …' (John 3:16). 'Greater love has no man than this, that he lay down his life for his friends' (John 15:13). So also it followed, the righteousness of God, the goodness, kindness, grace, and mercy of God, all find their decisive, clearest expression at the cross.

The climactic point of the sermon for me, whatever may have been the preacher's intent, came when he turned to ethics. How does 'Christ crucified' relate to Christian moral practice? As I recall, Martin began to ask, 'What does the apostle Paul say to the immoral man, to the man who has united his body to a prostitute, who has become one flesh with her? He plants the cross right in the middle of his exhortation,' Martin insisted. 'You are not your own,' he shouted. 'For you have been bought with a price: therefore glorify God in your body' (1 Cor 6:20, NASB). 'Bought with a price.' Why should we refrain from immoral acts? Because we were purchased by Christ at the cross, at the cost of his own precious blood. Consequently, *we are no longer our own* (1 Cor. 6:19).

It was one of those moments for me, something like a revelation from God. The centrality of the cross was clear in a way that it had never before been. 'Nothing but Christ crucified' does not mean that we repeat the same gospel facts every time we preach, with soul-suffocating monotony.

Rather, Jesus Christ is the centre around which all of Scripture revolves, and the cross is the hub around which all Christian practice turns. He is found in 'all the Scriptures,' as Jesus demonstrated to the disciples in the greatest survey of the Bible ever taught (Luke 24:27). 'Moses … wrote of me,' Jesus says of the Old Testament (John 5:46). 'Him we proclaim,' the apostle Paul says simply (Col. 1:28).

Christian *theology*, then, is cross- and Christ-centred. Christian *ethics*, likewise, are cross- and Christ-centred. 'Follow in his steps' of selfless sacrifice, says the apostle Peter (1 Pet. 2:21). 'Have this attitude which was in Christ Jesus,' the attitude of looking out for the interests of others and regarding others as more important than oneself, the attitude that is obedient even unto death (Phil. 2:5ff.). 'Just as I have loved you,' Jesus says, 'you also are to love one another' (John 13:34; 1 John 2:16). 'Christianity *is* Christ,' as a book title of a previous generation succinctly put it. He is the Alpha and Omega of all that we know and all that we have to say.

The point

Note that we have not yet discussed the point of the passage, only its context and far-reaching implications. The point is, 'You are not your own.' One can scarcely imagine a more counter-cultural message than this for the twenty-first century. If there is one message that the modern world screams, it is this: *I* am my own. I am my own to do with myself *whatever I wish* to do. Life is about *me*. I define myself. I determine my identity. I am accountable to no one. I am responsible to no one. I answer only to myself—not to my parents, not to my family, not to my school, not to my church, not to society generally, not to an external moral code, not even to God! Authenticity requires this outlook. I have to be myself, and what I am is determined by me alone.

We speak today of the 'sovereign self.' Yet this thinking has been around for a long time. Call it the Popeye (the cartoon character) philosophy: 'I am what I am and that's all I am.' Get used to it. Decades ago the feminist book *Our Bodies, Ourselves* (1969, 1973) was published, advocating abortion rights, sexual liberation, and lesbianism. 'A woman's right over her own body' became the new mantra justifying the destruction of the unborn. Decades ago Sammy Davis, Jr. sang, 'I've got to be *me*,' that is, I am what I conceive and want myself to be and no one else's opinion matters. Similarly Frank Sinatra famously sang, 'I did it *my* way,' not some way imposed from without, not some standard other than my own. 'Have it *your* way,' burger joints promise. Going all the way back to the Greeks, the philosophy 'To thine own self be true,' has been around.[1] Go where your emotions, dreams, desires, impulses, inclinations take you. Liberate yourself from the expectations of others. 'Just do it,' whatever you may choose *it* to be. You

[1] The phrase is from Polonius in Shakespeare's *Hamlet.*

have no obligations beyond the obligation to be yourself, to be whatever you want to be. This is the message that our culture screams at us all day long, every single day.

At one level this can be sound advice: stop trying to be someone or something that you are not. Be yourself. Accept your limitations. Develop the gifts and abilities you have rather than fantasizing about becoming something else. Be content. Be real. Don't pretend. Every false philosophy has an element of truth without which it would not attract devotees.

At a more important level, this philosophy has left massive human wreckage strewn across the social landscape. 'To thine own self be true' really means 'to thine own *feelings* be true.' Do what suits you. Do what pleases you. Do what fulfils you, what satisfies you. Follow your emotions. Fulfil your desires. Don't bother to take anyone else into consideration. Abandoned children and abandoned spouses have been the victims of this selfish pursuit of 'authenticity' by husbands, wives, and parents. Churches have been the victims of ministers pursuing their own happiness as they had affairs with those who were their true 'soulmates.' Broken promises and betrayal of trust are the legacy of the philosophy of 'I am my own.' The Christian life begins on the opposite foundation. 'I am *not* my own,' it says. This ethic rests on two foundations.

Creation

First, we belong not to ourselves but to our Maker. We did not create ourselves. Life is a gift to us from our Creator. God made us for his purposes with a specific intention and design. We are obligated to fulfil that design. This is foundational for what the apostle Paul writes in our text in 1 Corinthians. Human nature is a given. There is that which is consistent with human nature, which fits it, which is compatible with it, and that which is not. When a man and a woman unite in sexual union, it can never be considered casual or inconsequential. They are bound together in a manner that is physical, yet never merely physical. They become 'one flesh':

> *Or do you not know that he who is joined to a prostitute becomes one body with her? For, as it is written, 'The two will become one flesh'* (1 Cor. 6:16).

The apostle cites Genesis 2:24: 'The two will become one flesh.' He takes us back to the creation narratives of the book of Genesis and God's intention and design. A one-flesh reality results whenever that union occurs, an effect of deep significance. This leads to the horrifying realization:

> *But he who is joined to the Lord becomes one spirit with him* (1 Cor. 6:17).

But, realize, he says, you who are uniting physically with a prostitute are also united by faith to Christ. A believer joined to a prostitute with his body simultaneously is joined to the Lord in his spirit. Christ and the 'members' of Christ are being dragged into this moral cesspool (1 Cor. 6:15). This leads further to the urgent exhortation:

> *Flee from sexual immorality. Every other sin a person commits is outside the body, but the sexually immoral person sins against his own body* (1 Cor. 6:18).

One cannot do whatever one wishes with one's body. One must do what God has designed for the body or else one 'sins against [one's] own body,' the apostle hinting ominously at unelaborated consequences as a result of violating the purpose for which God made us physical beings.

Recognize that we live in a crazy moment in history. The philosophy of 'I am my own' is the cultural air we breathe, the cultural water we drink. It has led to normalizing of homosexuality, which violates design, and transgenderism, which absolutely rejects design.

Periodically whole civilizations may be struck with blindness. We know this in the South of the United States of America. The Jim Crow system was an extended period of insanity regarding race in the Southern states. The Salem Witch Trials were a short but intense period of blinding hysteria in seventeenth-century New England. So also was the pre-school childcare hysteria of the 1990s, involving the McMartin preschool in Manhattan Beach, California, and the Fells Acres Day Care in Malden, Massachusetts, among others. Germany has a long and noble history of unparalleled cultural achievement. It is the land of Luther, of Bach and Beethoven, of Frederick the Great, and of Mercedes-Benz and BMW, of academic leadership in nearly every field of scholarship. Yet for twelve years Germany was swept up in political insanity under Adolf Hitler and the Nazis. It happens, and it is happening right now in Western civilization.

The 'transgender moment,' as it has been called, is a moment of moral and cultural madness. Biological boys, because they think they are girls, are being allowed to use girls' restrooms and locker rooms. Boys are being allowed to compete in girls' athletic events. Parents are being ordered by the courts to use their child's preferred pronouns even if those pronouns are the opposite of their biological sex, or risk the right to the custody of their own children. Adolescent and even pre-adolescent children are having sexual organs surgically altered and/or removed and are undergoing drug therapy to either suppress or promote gender development. It is crazy, but it also is the logic of the philosophy of *me*. I belong to me and no one else. I do what I wish to do.

The Christian answer is, I do not and never have had the right to do with my body whatever I wish. If I defy the design of nature and nature's God, I displease God and in the natural course of things I will suffer negative consequences. I cannot deny reality and expect to thrive. I will receive in myself the 'due penalty' of my error (Rom.

1:27). The potter has the right over the clay (Rom. 9:20-24). God has the right to tell us how we are to live. Our obligation is to trust him and seek to honour him in all our thoughts, words and deeds, so that whether we eat, or drink, or whatever we do, all we do is to the glory of God (1 Cor. 10:13). Our obligation is to align our bodies and ourselves with God's will as revealed to us in his word. I am not my own.

Redemption

For Christians, this denial of self-will goes deeper. Not only am I not my own because I didn't make myself, but I am not my own because I didn't save myself.

> *Or do you not know that your body is a temple of the Holy Spirit within you, whom you have from God? You are not your own, for you were bought with a price. So glorify God in your body* (1 Cor. 6:19-20).

Because we are indwelt by the Spirit of Christ, we are temples of the Holy Spirit. Our bodies are sacred ground. Our bodies must not be profaned by immoral behaviour. Further, we have been 'bought with a price.' Jesus gave his life as a ransom for ours (Matt. 20:28). He paid the slave-price necessary to free us from bondage to sin (note: we never were our own; we were the slaves of sin). He paid the wages of sin through his death (Rom. 6:23). He redeemed us (again, this is the language of the slave market) from slavery (Rom. 3:24; Col. 1:14).

The result is, we now have a new owner. We are now God's slaves, slaves of righteousness (Rom. 6:16-23). He owns us twice over. He made us and he purchased us. We are not our own. We were 'bought with a price.' We belong to him. This means that our desires are secondary. This means that our dreams are secondary. This means that what pleases me takes a back seat. This means that *I* am secondary. My life is not my own, not if I am a Christian. I surrendered my life when I received Christ. This theme is repeated so unmistakably in the New Testament that it is surprising that we continue to miss it. Jesus says to all of his disciples,

> *If anyone would come after me, let him deny himself and take up his cross and follow me. For whoever would save his life will lose it, but whoever loses his life for my sake will find it* (Matt. 16:24, 25).

To take up the cross is to die to oneself. We must 'lose' our life, our claim to it, our right to it, our control of it, if we are to 'save' it.

When we become Christians, we present ourselves to God as sacrificial offerings, as the apostle writes:

> *I appeal to you therefore, brothers, by the mercies of God, to present your bodies as a living sacrifice, holy and acceptable to God, which is your spiritual worship* (Rom. 12:1).

What is placed on the altar—'our bodies, our selves'—is slain. We no longer live. When we became Christians, we presented ourselves as gifts to God to do with as he pleases, as he wishes, as he determines according to his goodness and wisdom. This is how the apostle Paul characterizes his own Christian experience:

> *I have been crucified with Christ. It is no longer I who live, but Christ who lives in me. And the life I now live in the flesh I live by faith in the Son of God, who loved me and gave himself for me* (Gal. 2:20).

One who is crucified no longer lives. This is obviously the case, nevertheless the apostle repeats the point so that we might not mistake it. 'It is no longer I who live.' My life now belongs to Christ. He 'lives in me.' He lives through me. I am his to use as he pleases.

He says again: 'And those who belong to Christ Jesus have crucified the flesh with its passions and desires' (Gal. 5:24). We have our passions. We have our desires. We have our feelings. For many people these are sovereign. I am only true to myself if I follow them. Otherwise I am being inauthentic. I am not being real, I'm a fake, a fraud, even a hypocrite if I am not being true to my passions and desires. The sovereign *self* is led by its sovereign *feelings*. The apostle says to Christians not only are we not following them, we have crucified them. They are no longer a factor. They count for nothing. They are dead. What only matters is what God wants. His will alone counts.

Again: 'But far be it from me to boast except in the cross of our Lord Jesus Christ, by which the world has been crucified to me, and I to the world' (Gal. 6:14). The world appeals enticingly to our desires: the flesh and its sensual pleasures; the eyes and their attraction to beautiful and coveted things; the pride of life, of position, recognition, prestige, and power (1 John 2:15-17). The world seeks to seduce us with these things. However, says the apostle, we have been crucified to the world and the world to us. The world has no place in us. It is dead to us and we are dead to it. Why? Because I am not my own. I belong to Christ. He purchased me. I am his servant, his slave. My life belongs to him to do with as he pleases. This is the Christian life. What he commands, we obey. What he says, we believe. Where he sends, we go. What he sends, we accept, no, we embrace and celebrate. This is what Elisabeth Elliot (1926–2015) called *The Great Surrender*. We are but branches of the True Vine who wish for nothing but to bear fruit for Christ's kingdom (John 15:1-5).

Understanding that we are not our own is a key to contentment, peace, and joy. Otherwise we will always be vulnerable to bitterness. Perhaps my life is difficult. There might be any number of reasons for this. Perhaps my health is poor. Perhaps I was born without the physical attributes I desire. Perhaps I was born into social circumstances not to my liking. Or perhaps I didn't have the educational opportunities I might have desired. We could go on. Yet here I am. I am a Christian. As I look at the circumstances in which God has placed me, I may be tempted with bitterness unless I remind myself, 'I am not my own.' I belong to Jesus. He may do with me whatever he wishes. I am ready to serve in whatever capacity he assigns.

* * *

We now conclude our first look at the texts that transform life. We have considered the Christ who invites us to that life; how we enter into it by grace through faith; how it is related to law, works, and struggle; and how Christ by his Spirit imparts the power to live for him.

Is this new life to be lived in isolation? Not at all. Indeed, we cannot live it alone. Our next volume will examine the texts that transform our understanding of the church, its tasks, its ordinances, its ministry, and our place within it.

———————

General Index

Scripture Index